BANNEKER

A Case Study of Educational Change

BANNEKER

A Case Study
of Educational Change

John A. Wilson

An ETC Publication

1973

CIP

Library of Congress Cataloging in Publication Data

Wilson, John Alfred, 1938–

    Banneker; a case study of educational change.

    Bibliography: p. 116

    1. Banneker Elementary School. 2. Performance contracts in education. I. Title.

LD7501. G316W54 372.1'2   72–13935

ISBN 0–88280–005–1 $7.75

Copyright © 1973 by ETC PUBLICATIONS
                  18512 Pierce Terrace
                  Homewood, Illinois 60430

Printed in the United States of America

1773435

ACKNOWLEDGEMENT

Any attempt to recognize all the people contributing to this study is bound to be inadequate and probably somewhat pompous; however, there are some who must be thanked.

The candor and openness of the personnel of the School City of Gary, the State Department of Public Instruction, the Gary Teachers' Union, and Behavioral Research Laboratories deserve recognition and my gratitude.

Much of the material used in this study was collected jointly with Jim Mecklenburger. The long hours of conversation we had about what it all meant contributed greatly to the analysis of that material.

Without both the patience and encouragement of my wife, Gay, and daughter, Heather, the study and the resultant manuscript would have been impossible.

J. A. W.

TABLE OF CONTENTS

TABLE OF CONTENTS

BANNEKER

A Case Study of Educational Change

ONE

BEGINNINGS

"George and I got to talking once," said Gordon McAndrew, Superintendent of Schools in Gary, Indiana, speaking of George Stern, then president of Behavioral Research Laboratories (BRL) of Palo Alto, California.

> This must have been a year ago, and somehow we got to talking about what we thought about this whole 'accountability' notion. I said, kind of facetiously at the beginning, 'Tell you what. We'll contract with you to do this on a schoolwide basis, not just reading, but the whole shebang. Two conditions: One, it can't cost any more money than we're now spending, and two, you have to take the school as it now exists.' Out of that came a proposal.[1]

Significance of the Event

The proposal that resulted from the informal conversation cited above resulted in what has been referred to as the nation's boldest performance contract. The change that resulted from the performance contract between BRL and Gary for the operation of Banneker Elementary School is the focus of this book; more particularly, it is the changes that occurred in the various organizational structures that were affected by the performance contract project that are of most interest in this study. The structures that were affected by the change existed not only in School City, (Gary's school corporation is referred to as School City), BRL, the

3

BANNEKER

Gary Teachers' Union (GTU), but stretched to the Indiana Office of the State Superintendent of Public Instruction (OSPI).

In a paper produced for the editors of COMPACT, George R. Hall and James P. Stucker explained some of the reasons that HEW awarded a substantial contract to the Rand Corporation of Santa Monica, California, for the purpose of studying the phenomenon of Performance Contracting in U.S. education. They began their paper with the following:

> The performance contracting method was first applied to the education of public school students late in 1969. The ensuing publicity has generated widespread interest in the experimentation with this technique. Payment for services on the basis of student achievement, and the involvement of private, profit-oriented firms in classroom activities, have made performance contracting one of the most discussed and most controversial innovations in American education.[2]

"Gary's decision to farm out an entire school is unique, but the idea behind it—known to educators as 'performance contracting'—has in the past few months stirred many schools around the country."[3] In so saying, *Newsweek* noted that performance contracting has been a powerful idea in American education since the Texarkana project began in 1968, and, moreover, that the experience at Banneker is unique among a set of innovations.

One gets an indication of the national significance of the Banneker experiment from a later article in *Newsweek* when the project was under rather severe stress. The March 15, 1971, *Newsweek* suggests that:

> The resolution of Banneker's problems is of far more than local significance. The unprecedented BRL approach in Gary is being watched with intense interest by school officials throughout the nation as a way to introduce 'accountability' into education—a development that the Nixon administration has suggested might stimulate increased Federal aid to fiscally beleaguered U.S. school systems.[4]

4

Undoubtedly, the experiment at Banneker is of national importance and constitutes a definite change in a school. As G. R. Hall and M. C. Rapp pointed out in the Rand/HEW paper, *Performance Contracting in Education Report on Gary, Indiana,* "Banneker is different from the usual school. It is perhaps not as different as its originators wished, but there is no gainsaying that it is a significant departure from the conventional Gary school."[5] The change that occurred is carefully described in this book.

Hall and Rapp concluded their report by indicating that:

> Whatever the final outcome of the Banneker program, it should go down in educational history as one of the boldest and most interesting educational experiments in the United States. It deserves the attention of everyone interested in the current educational scene.[6]

Significance of the Study

There exists in education today a serious need for careful description and analysis of change in educational organizations. Seymour Sarason pointed out that:

> . . . we simply do not have adequate descriptive data on the ways in which change is conceived, formulated, and executed within a school system. Obviously, there are many different ways in which it comes about, with differing degrees of success and failure, but it has hardly been studied.[7]

And as Vernon Smith pointed out in *Changing Schools:*

> In spite of sincere intentions, massive funding, and earnest efforts, schools are not improving today, and indeed, may be getting worse. The single most positive result of the change efforts of the sixties is that we learned that we don't know how to change educational institutions.[8]

Maslow suggested that in most experimental programs, "we wind up with a retrospective story of the program, the faith, the confident expectations, but with inadequate accounts of just what was done, how, and when, and just what happened and didn't happen as a result. . . ."[9]

In the introduction to a major work, Havelock, *et al.*, indicated they

> were disappointed to find *so few case studies.* Of the thousands of dissemination and utilization events that take place each year, it is unsettling to find so few documented in such a way that others could learn from them. This deficiency in the literature was one of the factors that thwarted our efforts to code, analyze, and compare utilization processes across studies and fields. Each investigator, in effect, has his own special interests or his own special point to make, and few appear to be motivated simply to report what happened in specific utilization events.[10] [emphasis theirs]

In addition to the gross inadequacy of case materials, the problem of understanding change in education is exacerbated by the educator's characteristic disinterest in the organizational aspects of the educational enterprise.

Bidwell commented that the study of schools as organizations has been, at least, rare, and regrets that:

> Few students of organizations have turned their attention to schools, and few students of schools have been sensitive to their organizational attributes. To understand what schools are like as organizations—what their characteristic structures, processes, and functional problems are—we now must rely on empirical work, much of which was not explicitly directed toward these questions or was narrowly focused on some subsystem, process or activity within the school, without being informed by a more general conception of the school as an organization.[11]

Bidwell pointed out that as a result of what was said above, ". . . this empirical literature is fragmentary and discontinuous,"[12] and at the conclusion of his attempt in that chapter to ". . . move toward a formulation of the organizational character of schools . . . ,"[13] he summarized his efforts with:

> The attempt here has been made to suggest some possible dimensions of a framework for studying schools as organizations. The ideas advanced await new empirical evidence. Hopefully, this evidence will come from research including many more studies than presently exist concerned with the actual functioning of schools and school systems. Studies using direct observation, informants, and the analysis of documents are especially needed. Ratings of others' behavior or judgmental nominations which to date have been the principal sources of material on school operations, are weak substitutes for phenomenological data. Moreover, the attitudes of school personnel, about which we are now best informed constitute only a portion of the complex of variables which bear on the operation of school organizations.[14]

Sarason, quoted earlier, corroborates Bidwell when he points out a ". . . growing awareness that we know far less about the 'actual functioning of schools and school systems' than we have realized."[15]

There is a need to study schools that are in flux, and a need especially to study their organizational aspects because of the growing concern with finding efficacious methods and techniques for causing change in schools. We need to know whether the organizational structures can absorb new changes, making the necessary accommodations, or whether they must reject the change in a way similar to a human body rejecting a transplanted organ.

The fact that a school can be studied while in the throes of significant change will indeed make more visible its regular organizational works. Those structures are, in many cases, under attack when significant organizational change is occurring. This necessitates reaction from the various structures within the school and indeed, those outside that are affected by, or, in turn, affect the school. Change requires that potential power be exercised, and in that way become visible.

One other factor that makes a school undergoing major organizational changes important to one interested in the organizational structures within and surrounding a school, is the much higher frequency of important decisions associated with the changes. This increased rate of decision making, when coupled with the necessity for vested interests to exercise the power they hold, makes it much easier to identify both power sources and the organizational structures through which the power is exercized.

The school that is undergoing major organizational change is excited in the same sense the electrons in a glowing filament are excited, and in the same way as the filament, that school and its organizational structures become visible.

Procedures Used to Gather Data

The methods used in gathering the data to describe this organizational change included what Scott has referred to as " . . . 'field methods' that "include all the kinds of techniques which have been employed to examine behavior in naturally occurring groups—human beings 'on the hoof'—as opposed to studies of *ad hoc* groups conducted in the laboratory."[16] Scott goes on to point out that a field study might include "such diverse methods as interviewing, observation, and the analysis of documentary materials or other group products."[17]

Donald J. McCarty and Charles E. Ramsey, in their book, *The School Managers, Power and Conflict in American Education,* in explaining the methods they used to study power in educational systems, spoke to the problem of rigor in data collecting in the following way:

> Our own criticism of current methodology in the study of power and conflict is that it is far less rigorous

than even the comparatively poor methodology of the behavioral sciences generally. With this we are confident none of the critics or researchers in the field would disagree. But to develop more sophisticated techniques, structured questions, and statistical analysis in an area in which so little is actually known would be premature. At this point, a preferable strategy is to develop whatever understanding can be gleaned from studies using techniques bordering on the intuitive, be as honest as possible about methodology, and 'take the lumps' from anticipated critics.[18]

If anything, the study of organizational change in education is even more in infancy than the study of power and conflict. Therefore, the data used in this case study of educational change were gathered with methods, in many cases, "bordering on the intuitive," because the groups involved in this project were indeed human beings "on the hoof." We won't be startled if there turn out to be some "lumps" to take.

This investigation included many trips to Banneker and the central offices in Gary, many interviews with not only the key personnel at Banneker, but those in School City, the Gary Teachers' Union, and the Indiana Department of Public Instruction as well. Important documents having to do with the project have been collected, as well as virtually all that was written (and there has been much) about the performance contract in Gary. The investigation included attendance at national conferences and workshops having to do with performance contracting in general. This writer has co-authored two articles about this contract[19, 20] as well as other articles about other sites[21, 22] and performance contracting in general.[23] This process not only enabled this writer to establish dialogue with persons important in the general movement of performance contracting, but served to help establish the credibility of the investigation within the systems being investigated as well.

Most of the interviews were taped and later transcribed. The taped interviews were helpful in many ways and used in much the same way as McCarty and Ramsey indicated they used their own transcribed interviews: "The interviews were used in a manner analogous to the biologists' use of a microscope. They told us about events which had occurred; they were sources of data and were given consideration commensurate with their usefulness."[24]

The taped interviews were particularly useful in questioning persons having separate roles in the same organization, persons in different organizations, and the same person at different times, about a single event. Instances occur, in all those combinations, of differing perceptions of the same event.

Formal lists of questions were not developed for this book. In attempting to discern the structures within organizations and how those structures were affected by events, any question asked an individual must, it seems, be dependent not only on the formal position of the individual within the organization in question, the event in question, but also on the answer to any previous question as well (e.g., it would make little sense to ask a teacher what arrangements had been made regarding copyright for 'in-house' produced materials).

Organizing and Analyzing Data

This case study differed from the few case studies of change in education in that most studies having to do with change have been (to repeat Bidwell) "narrowly focused on some subsystem, process or activity within the school, without being informed by a more general conception of the school as an organization."[25] This study, however, was even more general than Bidwell suggested. It studied not only the school as an organization, but also how that organization interacted with other organizations. It studied how a school as an organization formed a suprasystem resulting from the affects by and on other organizations.

It is hoped that this book may serve two basic purposes. The careful description of the organizational aspects of this innovative project should prove of value to those future researchers attempting to move toward a more complete understanding of the organizational nature of schools. In addition, it is possible for practitioners to use the case materials provided to make a tentative analysis of their own organizational structures with a view toward improving them.

The case materials were arranged more or less chronologically in Chapters Two through Five. In Chapter Six, the tentative analysis of the organizations involved in this study relies, to a large extent, on the Configurational Theory of Innovation Diffusion, developed by Harbans Singh Bhola. This theory, which Havelock, *et al.,* have referred to as ". . . a most significant step toward a general science and engineering science of D and A processes,"[26] is briefly outlined therein.

----

[1] Mecklenburger, J. A., and Wilson, J. A., "The Performance Contract in Gary," *Phi Delta Kappan* LII:406-407, March, 1971.

[2] Hall, G. R., and Stucker, J. P., "The Rand/HEW Study of Performance Contracting in Education," p. 1.

[3] "Teaching for Profit," *Newsweek,* August 17, 1970, p. 58.

[4] "Banneker at Bay," *Newsweek,* March 15, 1971, p. 95.

[5] Hall, G. R., and Rapp, M. L., *Case Studies in Educational Performance Contracting,* p. 93.

[6] *Ibid.,* p. 94.

[7] Sarason, S. B., *The Culture of the School and the Problem of Change,* p. 20.

[8] Smith, V. H., "Alternative Schools: A Rationale for Action," *Changing Schools,* No. 002, 1972, p. 12.

[9] Maslow, A. H., "Observing and Reporting Educational Experiments," *Humanist,* January-February, 1965, p. 13.

[10] Havelock, R. G., *et al., Planning for Innovation Through Dissemination and Utilization of Knowledge,* p. 17.

[11] Bidwell, C. E., "The School as a Formal Organization," *Handbook of Organizations,* p. 972.

[12] *Ibid.*

[13] *Ibid.*

[14] *Ibid.,* p. 1018.

[15] Sarason, *op. cit.,* p. 229.

[16] Scott, R. W., "Field Methods in the Study of Organizations," *Handbook of Organizations,* p. 262.

BANNEKER

[17] *Ibid.*

[18] McCarty, D. J., and Ramsey, C. E., *The School Managers, Power and Conflict in American Education,* p. 241.

[19] Mecklenburger, J. A., and Wilson, J. A., "The Performance Contract in Gary," *Phi Delta Kappan* LII:406-410, March, 1971.

[20] Mecklenburger, J. A., and Wilson, J. A., "Behind the Scores at Gary," *Nation's Schools,* December, 1971.

[21] Mecklenburger, J. A., and Wilson, J. A., "Performance Contracting in Cherry Creek," *Phi Delta Kappan* LII:51-54, September, 1971.

[22] Mecklenburger, J. A., and Wilson, J. A., "The Performance Contracts in Grand Rapids," *Phi Delta Kappan* LII:590-594, June, 1971.

[23] Mecklenburger, J. A., and Wilson, J. A., "Learning C.O.D.: Can the Schools Buy Success?" *Saturday Review,* September 18, 1971, pp. 62-65, 76-79.

[24] McCarty and Ramsey, *op. cit.,* p. 247.

[25] Bidwell, *op. cit.,* p. 972.

[26] Havelock, *et al., op. cit.,* pp. 10-11.

TWO

THE AGREEMENT

The intent of this chapter is to chronicle the events leading up to the decision to enter into a performance contract. This decision was not made in isolation by the School City of Gary (Gary refers to its school corporation as School City) and Behavioral Research Laboratories (BRL) of Palo Alto, California. On the contrary, the fact that School City and BRL were considering such an arrangement evoked strong reaction from the Gary Teachers' Union and the Office of the State Superintendent of Public Instruction.

In addition to describing leading events, this chapter deals with the characterization of the change envisioned by BRL's proposal and attempts to gain some insight into the reasons behind both School City's and BRL's decision to enter the performance contract.

The intent of the performance contract in Gary was summarized in the proposal that BRL submitted to Dr. McAndrew and the Gary School Board:

Gary's Right to Learn Contracted Curriculum Center establishes, in one public elementary school of 800 students, an alternative model with the clear objective of raising each participating child to a specified level of academic achievement. The mechanism employed to achieve this objective is the temporary delegation of the total school operation to a private firm on a contractual basis. On mandate from the Board, the private firm, Behavioral Research Laboratories, will implement all the appropriate, proven techniques of instruction, staff development, community participation, and school management required to produce measurable results. If, over the course of three years, Behavioral Research Laboratories fails to achieve the desired results for any child, the company will return the fee it has received in payment for that child's education.[1]

Because of the apparent illegality of the "temporary delegation of the total school operation" to BRL, the final contract called for the Board to retain supervision and control as BRL undertook to "develop plans for organizing and staffing the Curriculum Center School for a minimum of 700 students to be created at Banneker Elementary School in Gary, Indiana (the 'Center').[2]

The contract detailed the consultative duties of BRL with statements such as, BRL shall:

> Develop a curriculum in accordance with Indiana law and regulations and with any additional standards adopted by the board;

> Conduct a training and development program for staff and community members in respect to the objectives, philosophy and methods of student centered instruction, differentiated staffing, non-graded curriculum and other techniques that will be used in the center;[3]

The contract went on to specify BRL's duties in regard to the operation of the center as:

> Commencing with the 1970-1971 school year and continuing throughout the 1973-1974 school year, BRL, under the supervision and control of the Board, shall plan the operation of the Center, using its best efforts in such plan to raise the achievement levels up to or above national norms in basic skills. The 1973-1974 school year, unless otherwise determined by the Board, shall be a transition period in which BRL's participation in the Center planning will be phased out in an orderly manner.[4]

One can note that the contract, while formally deferring control to the Board, portends both significant changes in the operation and a strong emphasis on the results of the education in terms of national norms. The contract also called for the company to be involved for a long time (four years) but to quietly disappear as the contract ends.

The contract went on to become more specific regarding BRL's services by delineating such things as:

Designate all instructional materials, equipment, and supplies, subject to Board approval and in accordance with Indiana law;

Use its best efforts to establish a system to promote maximum student achievement in language arts and mathematics: utilizing appropriate techniques of instruction, such as student centered instruction, differentiated staffing; and non-graded curriculum.[5]

The contract went on to specify what amounts to the total operation of the school, but with phrases indicating that the operation is "under the supervision and control of the Board" always in evidence.

The operation of the Center differed from the usual school operation in Gary, not only because some of the methods and techniques were different (e.g., a very heavy reliance on programmed instruction materials), but because the decision-making structure was different. There were no completely new techniques of instruction in use at Banneker, but many changes in emphasis had been made at once. As George Stern, then president of BRL told *The National Observer,* through the contract BRL "gained the clout to implement all our ideas."[6]

Perceptions of the Function of the Performance Contract

Donald Kendrick, the project manager for BRL, saw the contract as a solution to a widespread problem. He told interviewers

15

in the fall that there must be some way to "instill in (staff) the accountability to work toward meeting objectives" in "schools all over."

He went on to point out that BRL was ". . . always a consultant" but that in his opinion anyone was ". . . fighting a losing battle if you can't get everyone in [the] system to work." He saw the performance contract as helping solve that problem.[7]

Dr. Brian Fitch, who replaced Kendrick in the spring of 1971, conceived the function of the contract in a little different manner. He suggested that ". . . the performance contract really provides a basis for negotiations between independent systems developers and school people." He went on to say about this particular contract that:

> What BRL said is, it's responsible, it feels responsible, for the total system development, but it's not just company materials, (BRL) realizes that in order to individualize the system, you've got to do more than provide the materials, you've got to provide new cycles and new patterns of movement for children, new scheduling patterns and new staff patterns, and you've got to be able to pull these things together into a cohesive system. You're saying when you take a performance contract for an entire school, you're going to come up with a total system for that school.[8]

Dr. Otha Porter, then assistant to Superintendent Gordon McAndrew, saw the function of the performance contract as solving schools' problems with underachievement. In October, he said:

> When an organization tells you 'we think we can do something about that (underachievement in basic skills) and we'll guarantee the results,' then I think it would be criminal for the school system not to give them an opportunity.[9]

The perception that the performance contract might be a means for "systems companies to negotiate with schools" didn't fit with

Charles O. Smith's perceptions of the performance contract. Charles Smith was the president of the Gary Teachers' Union, and a vice-president of the American Federation of Teachers (AFT). In December, 1970, he said about the project that:

> Under the original proposal, BRL would have, in fact, operated the school and every facet of the school's operation, including hiring professional staff, custodial staff, secretarial staff, and they would have been employees of BRL, and BRL would have been totally responsible for the program.

In response to an unofficial Attorney General's opinion about the legality of total delegation, the contract was revised in order that BRL be retained as consultant. Of that revised contract, Smith said:

> In legal terms of the contract, they are only consultants to the program. In fact, they control the operation of the school. The contract is a kind of legal fiction to enable School City to do what School City wanted to do in spite of what the Attorney General told them.[10]

Gordon McAndrew saw the contract with the outside company desirable for two distinct reasons. First, the economic guarantee of success or money back is possible only with an outside party. McAndrew saw this as important in getting the symbolic commitment to "shape up the system." Beyond the need for the guarantee and the commitment, he saw a more subtle force that could be provided from the outside more easily than it could internally. He suggested that he could have hired expert personnel to change the system from within, but that there was a problem involved that goes beyond knowledge of techniques of education that he illustrated in the following way:

> It's not only the (school's) written regulations and the state regulations that make change difficult, it's also the institutional inertia; it's not a matter of whether

you're forbidden to do something by union agreement, but whether you have the positive thrust to go ahead and do it. I had an experience with one guy who used to work with me, who came in here—a very bright guy, with all kinds of ideas—and he found himself very frustrated; he'd never worked in a public school bureaucracy. He said, 'It's not that it's forbidden, but when I talk to somebody about doing something new or doing something different, I'm smothered with kindness, but nothing happens. I can't make the beast move.'[11]

Precursors of Conflict

There are several implications in the proposal, the contract, and the perceptions of the function of the contract that set the stage for unavoidable conflict and organizational strain. The first was the idea that someone will have the "clout" required to "make the beast move." The "total systems approach" the proposal speaks of, implied changing many components of the system at the same time, and, in itself, was bound to be unsettling for individuals accustomed to an institution that changed little from year to year.

The different roles for teachers, students and materials, implied by statements in the proposal, set the stage not only for conflict arising among those immediately affected, but for conflicts with regulations and expectations of those outside the immediate system as well. For instance, state law, rules, and regulations regarding instructional materials are based on the traditional role of the textbook as an aid to teacher and student, while programmed instruction takes on the role of teaching. The student's traditional role is as a receptor of instruction, and in that role evaluation is used primarily to determine his value as good receptor. In a systems approach, as suggested in the proposal, at any rate, the student is at the center of the operation. Evaluation is used to diagnose any difficulties the student might have so as to enable the system to correct them with prescription of activities, rather than using evaluation for its traditional judgmental function.

Changes in staffing to patterns that rely more heavily on paraprofessionals and less strongly on certified teachers are not calculated to produce joy and acceptance in the halls of a teachers' union.

Even when the ideas and values of the institution are not displaced, semantic difficulties can cause conflict. "People who talk of management: 'cost-effectiveness', 'needs assessment' and 'product emphasis' rouse hostility in people who talk of 'the whole child', 'individual differences', '*my* classroom' or 'the learning process.' "[12]

McAndrew as Sponsor

"Inasmuch as our superintendent is a swinger and we deal with organizations that swing, we said, we've had (BRL's) Project Read for three or four years, it'd be a good idea if you guys took over a school."[13]

While the above statement, made by a Gary school official is obviously oversimplified, it does point out the central role of the superintendent in the events that produced the Banneker project.

The Rand study indicated that in every project they studied, one person stood out as the 'sponsor' of the project. Gordon McAndrew was obviously this sponsor in Gary.

Innovation in education was most assuredly in character for McAndrew. Before assuming the superintendency in Gary, he was Director of the Learning Institute of North Carolina. He was more than willing to examine the assumptions of conventional education, particularly where he found failure in conventional education. He wrote about another Gary project in *Educational Leadership,* saying that:

> . . . if a program which includes reading *Dick and Jane* and *Silas Marner* produces children with a 50 percent dropout record in the inner city and in some large urban areas in the United States, something has *got* to be wrong with the educational process.[14] [emphasis his]

Elsewhere in the same article, he revealed feelings about education in saying:

19

> We in the Gary School System want to take education out of its tuxedo and put it in dungarees. We want to grab the three R's by their arthritic ankles, turn them upside down, and shake out the stiff-necked conventions and meaningless rote of years. In effect, we want to stop 'processing children' and begin 'educating them'.[15]

One of the methods chosen in Gary to "shake out the stiff-necked conventions" was the performance contract with BRL.

After the discussion McAndrew had with Stern about the idea of BRL taking over an entire school on a contract basis, he proposed the idea to his board. "I recommended it and the board said 'Go, and work out this kind of thing.' They left up to me the details, the timing, and how you do it. At that point we hadn't even chosen the school. It was just an idea they were approving in principle."[16]

The Board Makes a Decision

The Board was ready to accept McAndrew's recommendation for several reasons, not the least of which was the underachievement in basic skills of Gary's students.

McAndrew pointed out that, "In 28 of our 33 elementary schools the average student leaves sixth grade performing below level in reading and mathematics."[17] At a press conference to announce the opening of the project, the Board president, Dr. Alphonso D. Holliday, stated:

> This contract was negotiated because of the gross underachievement of our children. The parents of the children attending Banneker feel that the Contracted Curriculum Center concept will insure that every one of our children will have the opportunity to learn.[18]

On another occasion, Holliday was somewhat stronger in his statement, "When you're at the bottom, all you can do is look up and try something different. We must be willing to be pioneers and no longer say that our children can't learn."[19] Holliday also saw strong implications in the project for school boards and others.

> If the Gary program works, it represents a breakthrough for the entire country because it offers a way of educating children successfully within the limitations of the tax base available for this purpose. The public will pay a good deal for education if it can be shown that the money is well spent. Until now, this has not been the case. The idea of performance contracting makes the educational establishment uneasy. They can't attack it directly, but they can challenge it on the basis of legal technicalities and union contracts. These are familiar ploys that in the long run can't obstruct success.[20]

It might be pointed out that this statement was published after the union in Gary had threatened to strike, then instituted a grievance procedure, and after the state had shown a reluctance to allow the project to begin.

Holliday's remarks elsewhere in the same *American School Board Journal* article give further indications of hardened positions:

> As a board president, I soon realized that you could either decide to improve the calibre of the education program—or get off the board. You can't in good conscience be a rubber stamp for continuing educational practices that are not working.

> . . . I think the public likes the fact that as a board we make decisions on key issues. We don't 'committee' problems and study them to death. We want the public to know where we stand—because people, not teacher groups, should control the schools.

> School boards must stand their ground for what is best for kids in their system no matter who is doing the complaining. Too many boards tend to be intimidated

by teacher unions or associations that know how to use pressure and smear tactics that really hurt. If they want to save public education, board members must dig in against mammoth educational costs when costs prove to be non-productive. Performance contracting seems likely to be one approach that deserves a fair chance.[21]

Assistant to the Superintendent, Dr. Otha Porter, suggested that it was not unusual to find an innovative program in Gary:

I would estimate that we have just about every major program other cities in the country have collectively, when outside groups came in they came in and operated under the assumption that we weren't doing anything. They thought they were starting from scratch, that we had been totally unsuccessful in our attempts to educate youngsters. Well, you know, that's not true. What we're saying is that, hopefully, we can do a significantly better job in the future than we have in the past.[22]

It deserves to be pointed out that the decisions of the board did not have the total unanimity implied by Dr. Holliday. Theodore Nering, the only white member of the board, had misgivings about the idea of a private contractor and particularly about the fact that the contract was let without competitive bidding. Nering described the decision and his misgivings:

I never voted against it, but I didn't vote for it. And the reasons I didn't vote for it were, for example, we didn't have any competition on this; we didn't have a chance to look at somebody else's program. I brought this up in a public meeting and Gordon McAndrew thought that this group (BRL) was most satisfactory, and from his observation and understanding there wasn't the need or the necessity to talk to someone else. I still thought we should have. I thought I, and even the rest of the board, did not really understand this program. I felt that the board didn't know enough about it, and I also felt the administration didn't know enough about it. They wanted to get the program started in the fall, to get the show on the road. But we weren't in the position of being sure of ourselves at the time we made our decision. But since this deadline had to be met, at least they felt it had to be met, the decision was made.[23]

Nering also pointed out during that interview that since the Board had become minority group dominated, he had not had a single motion of his receive a second.

In Gary, the mayor appoints the school board members. Gary's mayor is the prominent Richard Hatcher, one of the first black major city mayors in the country.

One of the administrators in Gary gave some indication as to why the Board made the decision to go ahead with the project in spite of Nering's assertion that ". . . we weren't in a position of being sure of ourselves when we made our decision." Assistant to the Superintendent, Otha Porter, said about the program:

> The unique thing about this program is that they are telling us that 'we can improve the quality of instruction at no additional cost.' So when a school system asks, 'Can we afford BRL?', the answer is YES, because it doesn't cost you any more.[24]

Porter also saw the guarantee as being very important to the idea of performance contracting:

> I don't know how other people might look at this, but as a practicing educator and maybe as a businessman, you just treat people differently when you're able to place a dollar value on that person. When Johnny sneezes you don't put him in the corner. You don't send him some place to rest up a period or keep him some place where he won't be receiving good instruction. You're going to try to analyze Johnny's problems, and you're going to try to design a program for Johnny and you automatically treat Johnny as if he were a student in a private school.[25]

In addition to shedding light on some of the reasons the Board was willing to step into the unknown, the above statement gives some insight into the reason for the strong reaction against the project by the Union. The attitudes about what goes on in conventional schooling implied by Porter's statement are bound to threaten a teacher's expectation of his role in the organization. One further statement that illustrates this attitude more directly is Dr. Porter's view of the minimum competency one should have as he finishes teacher training. He felt that with a bachelor's degree, one should at least be ". . . a good practitioner or a good technician. I like to think of a teacher as being a creative technician. Really, they aren't going to create that much of their own work, but at least, hopefully, the teacher will know how to use instructional materials as designed or planned."[26]

Union's Initial Response

The controversy between the Union and School City's administration that blossomed with the implementation of the project will be explored more fully later, but the initial reaction was one of distrust of the motives of both BRL and School City. Several Union members expressed the idea that in their opinion, BRL would rather hire "technicians than teachers."

The decisions leading to the signing of the contract were also suspect in the Union's view. When Gary Teachers' Union President Charles Smith was asked why BRL was awarded a sole source contract, he replied with a note of sarcasm, "Because I think BRL's merchandising methods were very successful."[27]

Smith went on to discuss big-business PR methods used by many publishers. He suggested that publishing companies hire teachers from one school to consult in other schools receiving goodwill because of the consulting fees paid. He concluded that part of the discussion with, "I just think it's totally indefensible, both the methods used by BRL and the methods employed by our own staff to select BRL."[28]

Why BRL?

To go back to an earlier quote of this chapter—"we've had Project Read for three or four years, it'd be a good idea if you guys took over a school."[29] —suggests that BRL and Gary School City were friends before the beginning of the project.

McAndrew remembers how BRL came to mind in considering ways to cope with student underachievement in Gary:

> The first thing that's important here is that the company with whom we're contracting has been in Gary on Project Read. Actually they were here before I got here. When I got here, they were doing some summer programs with seventh grade kids, underachievers.

> When I was looking around at the data on the results of various programs, the one program that seemed to show some glimmer was that one, the summer reading program using Sullivan materials. As a result of that, I thought we ought to try it a little more extensively. Therefore, last fall we put the Sullivan reading materials into half a dozen elementary schools. The evidence we have on this is pretty good. The data we have indicated, particularly in the primary grades, there was a significant difference in the achievement of the children. In the upper grades it wasn't any better, it wasn't any worse, so just on that dimension we're continuing it the second year.

> During the course of talking to BRL people about that I got to know the president of the company, a guy named George Stern.[30]

McAndrew and Stern became friends and together hatched the idea of a performance contract involving an entire school. When asked why no competitive bidding, McAndrew replied:

> I did talk with a couple of other firms. They indicated that they would not be interested. They said they didn't want to do it on a whole school basis, which was the only way I wanted to do it. I think the other thing was I knew something about the BRL program. Now, I think also, in talking with Stern and some of his people, they kind of grabbed the concept as well as I did.[31]

BANNEKER

Otha Porter thought "BRL was our only contact." He admitted that "Some people have criticized us for that," but went on to defend School City's position by saying that "BRL more or less tailor-made a program for us."[32]

Charles Smith's contention on this point that the contract was due to BRL's "merchandising" is already known.

BRL's Decision

The simple "free enterprise" idea that BRL would take on the project because of the money to be made on site, doesn't seem to be a plausible explanation to either the principals in School City or the Union.

Although George Stern somewhat cautiously suggests that he thinks BRL can make money on site, even he equivocates with ". . . it's planned so we can—but we also expect to spend beyond our budget if that is what it takes to improve the program."[33] Going beyond the budget doesn't constitute a denial of the business ethic; it merely suggests that the stakes for BRL are higher than only making a profit on this site.

He goes on to imply a developmental role for the project:

> At Banneker we've been able to use the best from a number of different programs we've piloted at other places. We've also tried a few new things, such as a truly flexible schedule that is hard to implement in a conventionally run school. We knew it would work and it has. The key to our program, or to any individualized program, is to diagram each child's starting skills and move from there. The thing to keep in mind at Banneker is that we've changed the learning environment in part by *altering staffing* so that it is no longer possible to do some of the wrong things that were being done before.[34]
> [emphasis supplied]

Nicholas McDonald of the School City central staff didn't think that it looked much like BRL could make money on the Banneker site. He pointed out that they planned to bring in

26

consultants "at considerable expense" and that BRL is paying for evaluation of the project. McDonald suggested that there might be savings in salaries but "it doesn't look that way."[35]

In May, 1971, McAndrew said, "I'm fairly convinced that there is no way that BRL is going to earn any kind of substantial profit in terms of the operation of it (the project)."[36] He went on to suggest reasons why BRL might take on the contract even with chances for profit slim at best. "I'm sure there are various ways in terms of their corporate structure they can write off things as developmental costs."[37]

Otha Porter had a more straightforward analysis of why BRL might be willing to spend more money on the project than they will take in:

> For example, they've already (October 1970) received more than a million and a half dollars in free publicity. I could call this an investment. Someone might say 'what if they're successful?' Well, if they're successful, they're going to shake up education in this country. . . . Not only that, if they're successful, they'll (materials) be in big demand.[38]

Charles Smith analyzed BRL's reasons in much the same manner as Porter. Smith suggested that BRL accepted the contract ". . . mainly to publicize their materials throughout the country." He also pointed out that BRL, being a young and relatively small company, is flexible but in his estimation more likely to become a big publisher than to take over very many schools.

Initial Reaction of the Office of the State Superintendent of Public Instruction

In BRL's proposal to the Gary Schools, they suggested that the mechanism to be used to achieve the objectives of the contracted curriculum center was the ". . . temporary delegation of the total school operation to a private firm on a contractual basis."[39] The proposal went on to say that BRL ". . . will implement all the appropriate, proven techniques of instruction, staff development, community participation and school management required to produce measurable results."[40]

When Gary officials took the proposal to the Office of the State Superintendent of Public Instruction in mid-June of 1969 and asked for approval as an experiment, they were told that such an experiment would require action by the Commission on General Education of the State Board of Education and the proposal should be formally submitted.[41]

When the proposal was submitted formally in late June, OSPI reacted to the "temporary delegation of the total school operation to a private firm" by requesting Attorney General Theodore L. Sendak's opinion as to the legality of the proposed contract. An Unofficial Advisory Letter from the Attorney General's office informed OSPI that the proposed contract would remove Banneker from the Common School System of the State. The Gary school officials received a copy of this letter, but that failed to stop the project. The State Board of Education then asked for a meeting with the Gary school officials which was held on August 11, 1970. In this meeting, it was informally reported that attempts were made to dissuade Gary from continuing with the project.

It was reported that State Superintendent Richard D. Wells offered $20,000 "no strings attached" to Gary to hire a BRL consultant if they would forego the project.

When Dr. Porter was questioned about that offer, he admitted that it was made to him, but:

> When you get a consultant, there are all those strings attached, guidelines and so on; no one is going to give you money with 'no strings attached.' Another thing is it would not fit in with our contract (with BRL). Let's put it like this: that idea was rejected.[42]

When pressed as to the source of the rejection, Porter said that it was he who rejected the idea. When pressed further as to whether the board was informed of the offer from OSPI, he replied that:

> You might say I participated with the board in the development of the current (project) and so I acted

(in the spirit) of the board. I accept all the blame for (the rejection of Wells' offer). Now, if he'd given me $20,000 to go into another school, I would have accepted that.[43]

When OSPI learned that a modified contract had been submitted to the office of the Attorney General but not to OSPI, John Hand wrote a letter to Attorney General Theodore L. Sendak requesting his opinions as to the legality of the modified contract. Hand's letter of September 15, 1970, was answered by Deputy General Thomas L. Webber in a letter that concluded by saying:

> As the school and program referred to in your letter must necessarily be a part of the Common School System of the State, it is subject to the Rules and Regulations duly promulgated by the State Board of Education, the State Superintendent of Public Instruction and other State Officers and agencies given authority by statute on public school matters.
>
> Since this is an unofficial advisory letter, the same is merely the opinion of the writer, and is not to be construed as being a precedent of the office of the Attorney General.[44]

Wells decided to form a committee to study the project to be sure it was within the "Rules and Regulations duly promulgated by the State Board of Education, the State Superintendent of Public Instruction . . ." and advised McAndrew not to sign the contract.

According to John Hand, on September 22, 1970, he tried to reach McAndrew by telephone in order to read Wells' letter to him. He was told McAndrew could not be reached but he was able to reach Porter. He said he read Wells' letter to Porter twice, asking him to be sure McAndrew was informed of its contents before the scheduled Gary School Board meeting that night. Hand said he found out on September 23, 1970, that the contract was signed on the night of September 22, 1970, and that the project had effectively been in operation since late August, 1970.[45]

Gordon McAndrew, in January, 1971, summarized the beginnings of the project:

> Now one of the decisions we had to make, of course, was should we go for broke and see if we could start this fall, or should we wait another year, because we were in the spring and a lot of planning still had to be done. And there was the whole question, of course, of the reactions of both the teachers' union and the state authorities. I talked to the teachers' union before the proposal ever went to the board. My feeling was that they were not particularly hot about the idea. What I wanted them to do was join with us, because I knew there would be questions of contract involved with this. For their own reasons they did not really feel they should go along. Now I think what they've accused me of is ramming it down their throat. That's OK too. Be that as it may, we started in the fall and of course we have had all the hang-ups with the state and the union that we anticipated.[46]

---

[1] "The Right to Learn Contracted Curriculum Center," A proposal submitted by Behavioral Research Laboratories," 866 United Nations Plaza, New York, New York, June 1, 1970, p. 8.

[2] Agreement between Behavioral Research Laboratories and Board of School Trustees of the School City of Gary, Indiana, signed September 22, 1970, p. 3.

[3] *Ibid.*

[4] *Ibid.*, p. 4.

[5] *Ibid.*

[6] Anderson, Monroe, "Private Company Runs a Public School to Boost Kids Learning," *The National Observer,* October 26, 1970, p. 6.

[7] Stated by Donald Kendrick, Center Manager, Banneker Contractual Curriculum Center, in an interview with Orest Ochitwa in October, 1970.

[8] Stated by Brian Fitch, Center Manager, Banneker Contractual Curriculum Center, in an interview with the author in May, 1971.

[9] Stated by Otha Porter, Assistant to the Superintendent, School City of Gary, in an interview with the author in November, 1970.

[10] Stated by Charles O. Smith, President, Gary Teachers' Union, in an interview with the author in December, 1970.

[11] Stated by Gordon McAndrew, Superintendent, School City of Gary, in an interview with the author in May, 1971.

[12] Mecklenburger, J. A., and Wilson, J. A., "Learning C.O.D.: Can the Schools Buy Success?" *Saturday Review,* September 18, 1971, p. 62.

[13] Stated by Otha Porter, Assistant to the Superintendent, School City of Gary, in an interview with the author in March, 1971.

[14] McAndrew, Gordon, "Can Institutions Change?" *Educational Leadership,* January, 1970, p. 358.

[15] *Ibid.*

[16] Stated by Gordon McAndrew, Superintendent of School City of Gary, in an interview with the author in January, 1971.

[17] McAndrew, Gordon, "Can Institutions Change?" *op. cit.,* p. 358.

[18] Office of Superintendent of Schools, Gary, Indiana, press release issued September 29, 1971.

[19] "Performance Contracting: Why the Gary School Board Bought It. And How," *American School Board Journal,* January, 1971, p. 21.

[20] *Ibid.*

[21] *Ibid.*

[22] Stated by Theodore Nering, member, Gary Board of Education, in an interview with the author on January 11, 1971.

[23] Stated by Otha Porter, Assistant to the Superintendent, School City of Gary, in an interview with the author in October, 1970.

[24] *Ibid.*

[25] *Ibid.*

[26] *Ibid.*

[27] Smith interview, December, 1970, *op. cit.*

[28] *Ibid.*

[29] Porter interview, March, 1971, *op. cit.*

BANNEKER

[30] McAndrew interview, January, 1971, *op. cit.*

[31] *Ibid.*

[32] Porter interview, October, 1970, *op. cit.*

[33] "Performance Contracting: Why the . . . ," *op. cit.*

[34] *Ibid.*

[35] Stated by Nicholas McDonald, Assistant Superintendent, School City of Gary, in an interview with the author in December, 1970.

[36] McAndrew interview, May, 1971, *op. cit.*

[37] *Ibid.*

[38] Porter interview, October, 1970, *op. cit.*

[39] "The Right to Learn Contracted Curriculum Center," A proposal submitted by Behavioral Research Laboratories, June 1, 1970, p. 8.

[40] *Ibid.*

[41] Hand, J. S., Indiana Assistant Superintendent for Instructional Services, *Memorandum to the State Board of Education,* January 11, 1971.

[42] Stated by Otha Porter, Assistant to the Superintendent, School City of Gary, in an interview with the author in February, 1971.

[43] *Ibid.*

[44] Webber, T. L., Indiana Assistant Attorney General, Unofficial Advisory Letter to John S. Hand, September 17, 1970.

[45] Hand, J. S., *Memorandum . . . , op. cit.*

[46] McAndrew interview, January, 1971, *op. cit.*

THREE

THE FIRST FOUR MONTHS

In January, 1971, Gordon McAndrew pointed out that an early decision must be made about how to implement an innovative project:

> There is a kind of philosophic approach one has to decide on when you take on a new program. You can play it one of two ways. You know that whatever planning you do, there are going to be things that you're going to experience that you never anticipated. And the more different the program, the more different those things are going to be. You can sit and plan it, for a long time, and try to anticipate as many bugs as possible. That's one approach to take. Another approach is to say, well, you have to do some planning, but let's get going on it and let's get the bugs and work them out by experience rather than on paper.[1]

McAndrew chose the latter.

Services of BRL

The contract between BRL and School City of Gary spelled out the services that BRL was to provide in terms of "Planning Organization and Staffing of Curriculum Center" and in terms of the operation of the Curriculum Center.

The proposed services were of such an extent, and are described in such detail that the section of the contract that enumerates these services is reproduced, in full, in Panel I below.

BANNEKER

Essentially, the contract proposes that BRL will organize, staff, and train the staff of the Center. The contract further proposed that BRL will develop the curriculum, provide for community relations, provide the instructional materials to be used, and even provide for custodial services.

This section of the contract carries numerous references to the control of the Board and the necessity for being in accordance with Indiana law. These references were to figure in the battle with the Office of the State Superintendent of Public Instruction, described in Chapter Four. One would suspect they occur not only for legal reasons, but also to minimize the threat to the other systems involved (State and teachers' union by suggesting that the changes would not alter their role expectations to any great extent).

PANEL I

Nature of Services

(A) *Planning, Organization and Staffing of Curriculum Center*

Prior to the beginning of the 1970-1971 school year, BRL, as hereinafter more particularly set forth, shall develop plans for organizing and staffing the Curriculum Center School for a minimum of 700 students to be created at Banneker Elementary School in Gary, Indiana (the "Center"). BRL, in all matters under supervision and control of the Board, shall:

(1) Develop a curriculum in accordance with Indiana law and regulations and with any additional standards adopted by the Board;

(2) Meet with teacher, parent and community groups and conduct workshops and discussions

34

with respect to administration, organization and curriculum development;

1773435

(3) Conduct at least four community meetings in order to provide further information, determine parents' views and enlist support for the Center;

(4) Conduct a training and development program for staff and community members in respect to the objective, philosophy and methods of student centered instruction, differentiated staffing, non-graded curriculum and other techniques that will be used in the Center;

(5) Establish curriculum objectives, physical and organizational arrangements of the Center, staffing assignments and patterns, and procedures for maintaining individual student profiles;

(6) Arrange, with the Board's administrative staff, for the provision of instructional materials, supplies and equipment to be used in the Center, subject to applicable Indiana law;

(7) Direct intensive, pre-service training of staff, orienting the staff to the individualized student-centered approach to be used in the Center, including role-playing, sensitivity training, and individual interview techniques;

(8) Provide, subject to applicable Indiana law and working with the Board's administrative staff, manuals, films, video and audio tape equipment, and other materials required for staff development programs;

(9) Prepare a yearly calendar of activities connected with the Center, including staff develop-

ment programs, parent information and participation activities and a series of opportunities for other members of the Gary School community to observe and work in the Center.

(B) *Curriculum Center*

Commencing with the 1970-71 school year and continuing through the 1972-73 school year, BRL, under the supervision and control of the Board, shall plan the operation of the Center, using its best efforts in such plan to raise the achievement levels up to or above national norms in basic skills. The 1973-74 school year, unless otherwise determined by the Board, shall be a transition period in which BRL's participation in the Center planning will be phased out in an orderly manner. Specifically, but not by way of limitation, BRL shall in each school year perform the following services:

(1) Designate all instructional materials, equipment and supplies, subject to Board approval and in accordance with Indiana law;

(2) Use its best efforts to establish a system to promote maximum student achievement in language arts and mathematics; utilizing appropriate techniques of instruction, such as student-centered instruction, differentiated staffing; and non-graded curriculum;

(3) Carry on intensive staff development and in-service training with both professional and teacher personnel, utilizing latest techniques of staff development and emphasizing methods of formulating and achieving behavioral objectives, increasing achievement, and motivation of students and staff; improving work relation with colleagues and parents; and training personnel in the methods

and objectives of the Curriculum Center after BRL has been phased out of the program during the fourth year of this agreement;

(4) Diagnose, prescribe, monitor, and help implement an individualized educational program for each child;

(5) Present detailed plans for organizing instructional activities around a number of learning centers to which children will go to develop particular skills, with school staff members specializing in work at that center and at the direction of the Board assist in implementing such plans;

(6) Present detailed plans and implement detailed procedures to use individualized instructional materials so that the children progress at their own rates of speed, moving in and out of learning centers according to schedules set up in consultation with school staff members; and at the discretion of the Board and, in accordance with Indiana law, assist in implementing such policy;

(7) Prepare plans for directing the organization and control aspects of the Center, including arranging monthly evaluation of each child's progress and transmission of this information to the instructional personnel, arranging supervision of attendance and discipline and establishing procedures that will seek to free instructional personnel from clerical and recordkeeping duties;

(8) In cooperation with the Gary School Service Center, assist in maintaining all records and provide all information required by law;

(9) Make provisions, working with the Board's administrative staff, to provide clerical, health and

day-to-day custodial services of a quality at least equal to that provided in the other elementary schools in the School City. These services shall be purchased from School City or contractors approved by School City. The exterior and interior maintenance and repair of the Center shall be performed by the Board;

(10) Cooperate with School City in affording other School City teachers opportunities to visit and work in the Center as part of a city-wide staff development program;

(11) Use its best efforts to implement an effective and meaningful community participation program, sending brochures and newsletters to parents explaining the activities of the Center, disseminating news about the Center to local and other media where the Board or its administrative staff deems it desirable or necessary to the program, and providing parents with special materials to assist their children at home so as to stimulate learning and achievement.[2]

The duties described in the contract, along with the publicity about the program, carried the implication that BRL had a program which they would demonstrate during the project. The contract suggested this by detailing the services the company would offer in terms such as, ". . . present detailed plans and implement detailed procedures to use individualized instructional materials so that the children progress at their own rates of speed . . ." and "Diagnose, prescribe, monitor, and help implement an individualized program for each child."

The implications that BRL had a developed system that it could drop into a school that would do much better than the school had been able to do at providing kids with basic skills and at the same time "cost no more" were to provide critics with much ammunition to use in conflicts that developed. This was to prove particularly painful when the information began to become public that while the company had enthusiasm, expertise, some well-developed programmed materials for reading, and the capacity for developing a system with every chance of doing well at providing instruction in basic skills, it simply did not have that system developed and ready to go. The shift in the image of the project from one of demonstration of a system to one of the cooperative development of a system is described in Chapter Five.

The problem of over-promising by implication is illustrated in what one teacher had to say regarding the image provided him just by the name of the company and his frustration when he discovered that while perhaps they had better questions, they really did not have all the answers when they started the project.

> Last August my notion of a company with a name like 'Behavioral' 'Research' 'Laboratories' was something utopian. This was something I was really looking forward to. I said, 'Wow, these people must really understand what kids need. Take the kid where he's at, and work on his behavior.' It really enthused me. And when I found out that all this company had was its name, that they had no concept about kids or behavior it was so frustrating that it brought me incredibly low. Imagine that name, Behavioral Research Laboratories; I didn't think of big business when I heard that name. I thought it was some together company that could really do something for kids. I was really a mark, I guess. I was taken.[3]

It deserves to be pointed out here, that while this teacher had had his request for transfer written at one time, he decided not to submit it because of changes that took place in the program after January. He was again enthusiastic, albeit more cautiously, about the prospects for the program.

Staffing the Center

There are interesting differences in what the BRL proposal had to say about staffing, and the process for staffing called for by the contract. In order to be able to point out these differences, both the proposal and the contract are quoted here. First the proposal:

> BRL will begin procedures for recruitment, selection and hiring of the school staff on July 1. The company will provide a Center manager to direct the organization and non-academic affairs of the school. The manager will in turn hire a learning director, who stands in lieu of a principal. The learning director will select five curriculum managers, one each in the areas of reading and language arts, mathematics, social studies and foreign languages, science, and enrichment (arts and crafts, music, drama and physical education). Together, the learning director and curriculum managers will select fifteen assistant curriculum managers, who will be credentialed professionals, and twenty learning supervisors, who will be paraprofessionals. Three administrative aides and three custodians will also join the full-time Center staff. All members of the Center staff will become employees of BRL. Staffing and other personnel arrangements will be complete by August 1.[4]

The two items in this arrangement that are particularly noteworthy are: "The manager will in turn hire a learning director, who stands in lieu of a principal," and "All members of the Center staff will become employees of BRL." Both items imply strong control of the company over staff, particularly the manager over the learning director.

The contract came out looking somewhat different in these areas. The difference probably resulted from opposition by OSPI and the Attorney General's office to the complete delegation of authority and from union opposition to the teachers being in BRL's employ. Gary school officials also suggested that difficulties with such things as retirement benefits, accumulated sick leave, and teacher tenure, caused the contract to be different than the proposal regarding staffing. The contract's statement on staffing follows:

> 3. *Staff*
>
> BRL shall make recommendations for the selection

of the staff of Banneker Elementary School by the Board which it is contemplated shall (based upon an assumed enrollment of 800 students) consist of (i) a Center manager who will cooperate in directing the organization and non-academic affairs of the school and recommend selection of the learning director; (ii) the learning director who will have the status of a principal and who will be subject to control of the Board, select the curriculum managers, duly licensed as teachers, each in the area of reading and language arts, mathematics, social studies and foreign languages, science and enrichment (arts and crafts, music, drama and physical education). The curriculum managers, together with the learning director, will supervise choice of specific approaches and materials, and select the assistant curriculum managers; (iv) fifteen teachers serving as assistant curriculum managers who will direct learning supervisors and who will be licensed or provisionally licensed in accordance with Indiana Law; (v) twenty learning assistants who will be teachers' aides and who will, to the extent practicable, be chosen from parents of children attending Banneker; (vi) three School City custodians and (vii) two clerical employees. The staff personnel must have such licensing and accreditation as may be required under Indiana Law; and to this end, the Board will cooperate with BRL in the assignment to the Center of qualified and certified teachers to teach in the areas of reading and the language arts, mathematics, social studies and foreign languages, science and enrichment (arts and crafts, music, drama and physical education). All staff members who are School City employees shall remain such receiving compensation and related benefits from the School City of Gary. All such School City employees assigned to the Center shall remain under the supervision and control of the Board.[5]

BANNEKER

The contract still called for the Center manager to ". . . recommend selection of the learning director." This is not as strong as to "hire a learning director" but it does still seem to imply that should a conflict arise, the manager will have control over the learning director rather than the other way around.

Banneker Administration

It also seemed necessary to note the lack of any detailed job description for the center manager or learning director, though it did imply that the manager would handle the non-academic affairs of the schools and the learning director the academic affairs.

The proposal spelled out this division of authority with little more detail, suggesting that because of the manager, the "instructional personnel will be freed from all tasks that do not relate to the children's learning." And that:

> The Center manager and learning director will always be in close communication. The separation and overlap of their functions will evolve into a close working relationship and promote effective use of the Student Centered Instruction Techniques.[6]

The "close working relationship" did not evolve from the "separation and overlap of their function" and this became a significant factor during the first few months of the contract.

The Center manager that BRL provided was Donald Kendrick. Kendrick had been an Air Force and Lockheed system's analyst, and was bright and aggressive, though lacking in educational experience. The lack of educational experience might not have put him at much of a disadvantage, indeed it may have been an advantage in being able to see what had to be done for kids, had he resisted the tendency to speak in systemese rather than pedagese.

Clarence Benford was chosen as the learning director. Benford had been principal at Banneker, but had been at another school just prior to returning. Benford claimed that he came back to Banneker because the parents wanted him to, and that he did not know of the performance contract at the time he was reassigned to Banneker School. Benford's style was much softer and more retiring than Kendrick's.

The problems that resulted from having two men in a job that had heretofore been one man's job is more carefully explored later in this chapter and in Chapter Five.

The Center staff called for both in the proposal and in the contract is differentiated, with the curriculum manager's function approximating that of a department head, the assistant curriculum manager's job somewhat like that of a teacher, and the learning supervisor being an aide. McAndrew saw this as "one of the [different] elements of that program [vis-a-vis traditional school staffing] and I think the most significant."[7]

Attitudes Toward Staff

The fact that the teachers are referred to as "curriculum managers" is important. This implies not only a non-traditional role for the teacher, but a much more important role for instructional materials as well. The roles implied in the descriptions, and attitudes about the function of teachers expressed by some individuals of both the Banneker administration and School City central staff gave rise to problems, by violating the role expectations of educators holding a more traditional idea of a teacher's role.

It is easy to see how accusations that BRL would rather have hired "technicians" than "teachers" came about when at least one member of School City's central staff close to the project was heard to say, "I like to think of a teacher as being a creative technician."[8]

In an interview with Francine Moscove, Porter spoke to a question about the renaming of teachers by suggesting that their function has indeed been changed. "They more or less monitor learning, rather than involve themselves deeply in it, you see, just because you are working with, for the most part, programmed materials."[9]

The attitude that the teacher should be removed from the central point in schooling is also reflected in an interview of

BANNEKER

Donald Kendrick by Minnie Perrin Berson. When asked about the in-service training program, Kendrick replied that:

> Retraining a staff is difficult in concepts and methodology. We say, throw away everything you've done, because it's not going to be useful any longer. You are no longer the dictator in the classroom. The child learns by himself, so you get out of that problem. The system teaches.[10]

Later in the same interview, when asked about his background, he replied:

> Oh, I was afraid you'd ask me. Lockheed Missiles. I'm a systems analyst. I view things analytically. Keep out emotions. The idea is, let's fix this, and the children will come out different. When people have needs, the relationship disrupts. If you want money, it interferes.[11]

When pressed about threatened strike by teachers and aides, the reply was:

> You're always going to have tensions. Industry says, we want a job done. This is the difference. You don't have to love the guy next to you on the assembly line to make the product. He puts in the nuts, you put in the bolts, and the product comes out. Teachers can hate me and still get children to learn.[12]

To suggest that statements like this would tend to threaten the teachers' traditional central role in the process of schooling seems almost unnecessary.

The other factor at work in statements such as these is the referral to products, assembly line, keeping out emotions, etc. This kind of talk doesn't set well with the many educators who are fond of speaking of the whole child, teaching as love, self-fulfillment, etc. The role changes that teachers were required to make were definite, and certainly were central in the problems and confrontations that were later to threaten the project. The name changes for the teaching positions were more than a matter of rhetoric.

Managers

In contrast to the problem of role definition for the learning director and the center manager, School City did have rather complete job descriptions for Curriculum Managers, Assistant Curriculum Managers, and Learning Supervisors. The description of their responsibilities follows:

Responsibilities:

The Curriculum Manager will:

1. Supervise the Assistant Curriculum Managers in the development of the assigned instructional system. This will include the formulation of the specific instructional and/or behavioral objectives and co-ordination of all instructional materials to meet those objectives.

2. Direct and monitor the activities of the assigned Assistant Curriculum Managers, with the purpose of providing informal training and guidance in instructional techniques.

3. Coordinate the resources of the assigned curriculum areas, i.e., materials, personnel and time, in order to provide for the most effective learning condition for the students.

4. Provide support for the overall operations of the Center as described by the Center Director or the Learning Director.

5. Oversee and maintain proper learning environment.

BANNEKER

Responsibilities

The Assistant Curriculum Manager will:

1. Coordinate the resources of the assigned curriculum areas, i.e., materials, personnel and time, in order to provide for the most effective learning condition for the students.

2. Provide support for the overall operations of the Center as described by the Center Director or the Learning Director.

3. Oversee and maintain proper learning environment.[13]

Three items stand out in the above descriptions. The Curriculum managers were told to respond to the Learning Director or the Center Manager but were not told which kinds of issues were to be resolved by each; the descriptions were of management functions rather than the more traditional teaching roles; and there was no mention of the necessity to work with each individual student.

An interesting extension of the idea of giving school positions titles implying management functions was the renaming of the president of the Board to the Chairman of the Board, and the Superintendent of School City to the President of School City. The new titles were to be used only informally and internally as they weren't legal. McAndrew was cautious about reading too much into the renaming; he noted that people had said that it is a ". . . manifestation of a board that wants to put its operations on a businesslike basis," but "I wouldn't want to push that too far." McAndrew said he thought the name came out of a conversation he was having with a board member one day when the board member said, "I've never liked the name superintendent, it always sounds like the kind of a guy in charge of a penal institution." The Board member liked "president" and at the next board meeting the names were changed.[14]

46

The Gary Teachers' Union was bemused by the name change. Charles Smith related the Union's reaction to the name change in February, 1971.

> I ruled out of order last night a motion that henceforward, for local purposes, the president of the GTU be known as the superintendent of the Gary Teachers' Union but for all official purposes, we would continue to refer to the head of the organization as the president. I ruled the motion out of order, although it was quite obvious there was a lot of sentiment for it.[15]

Learning Supervisors

The aides in Banneker were designed to serve at least two major functions. The first is pointed out in their job descriptions:

Responsibilities:

The Learning Supervisor will:

1. Monitor students' use of equipment and materials.

2. Assist in student evaluation in performing a given task that has been described in behavioral terms with a specific criterion.

3. Supervise activities such as listening centers, gaming, laboratory experiments, science or language arts resource centers.

4. Provide assistance to students assigned by the Curriculum Manager or Assistant Curriculum Manager in classroom instructions.

5. Be responsive to the assigned Curriculum Manager in providing support for implementing the instructional system.[16]

BANNEKER

This description might fit the usual use of aides except for the responsibility to provide assistance directly to students. The aides were clearly thought of in a broader role than only the teachers' aide. The role of the aide varied in practice, however, with the curriculum manager or assistant curriculum manager that the aide might be assigned to. As one teacher pointed out:

> Teachers have different concepts of what an aide is. A lot of teachers just have aides sitting around. There are a lot of things an aide can do; I can't get around to everybody. I watch what she's doing and if she does something wrong, I tell her (not in front of kids, but later). I never had an aide before, but I like the idea of it. But some teachers don't let their aide do anything, they have a kind of jealousy. I don't know why. An aide can never take the place of a teacher. What I mean is, the average person who is an aide doesn't want to be a teacher.[17]

The second major function of the aides was not as clearly spelled out in the contract. This function was to be the primary ingredient in the "community participation program" called for in the contract. When discussing the community participation program, McAndrew said, "The best manifestation of it is the fact that the learning supervisors, the aides are, I think without exception, indigenous to the community. I think that's the substance of it."[18]

Teacher Selection

In his letter of October 21, 1970, in reply to an inquiry by GTU President Charles O. Smith, Raymond V. Komenick, Director of Personnel for School City, stated that teachers were not apprised of or involved in the establishment of criteria used in the selection of Curriculum Managers. However, he did describe the process of selection and the criteria used in the selection in the following way:

48

The process used in selecting the personnel for positions as Curriculum Managers was based on teacher profiles that met the requirements for instructors as well as being complementary to the total staff of the Center. Each teacher's profile was based on:

1. Minimum of Master's Degree.

2. The desire to participate in an innovative demonstration program.

3. Their choice in the five curriculum areas.

4. Educational background with demonstrated continuous growth.

5. Professional experience, with knowledge of new instruction.

6. K–3 and/or 4–6 grade teaching experience.

7. Experience in the five curriculum areas.

8. Demonstrated ability to work cooperatively towards the major objectives.

These eight elements were evaluated in the order as shown above, thus describing the teacher profile. A selected teacher has placed high in all of these qualities as related to the uniqueness of the five curriculum areas. Assuming qualifications were equal, then combined School City and Banneker building seniority prevailed.[19]

Assistant Superintendent Otha Porter suggested that the teachers were selected by the Center Manager and the learning director although the Center Manager had the control. "The teachers were selected by Mr. Benford, the former principal of Banneker school, and Mr. Kendrick. Mr. Kendrick sort of had to have the final say, inasmuch as he represented BRL."[20]

In Gary, teachers have *building* tenure as well as school district tenure. Since the BRL program required fewer professional employees than Banneker had before the program, the question of who would get to stay was important to the Union. Sandra Irons of the Gary Teachers' Union saw Kendrick's role in teacher selection as more important than even Porter saw it. She said that the teachers were all called in and interviewed by Kendrick, but told nothing about pay or expectations except that they would be expected to attend in-service meetings. As she put it at the February AFT get-together in Chicago:

> All the teachers were interviewed, but none of them knew who would be hired. After that, after all had been interviewed, they received letters informing them some of them had been chosen, others were not. And with the letter to the people who were not chosen, there was a form that said, there are 19 vacancies in the School City, please state your first, second, third, and fourth preference. We have in our contract with the School City that no teacher shall be involuntarily transferred. But they weren't involuntarily transferred, they're saying now, they just took a choice of where they wanted to go.[21]

The involuntary transfer question was to remain a bone of contention between the Union and School City.

Curriculum Problems

Even though the community, Board, and Superintendent had expressed the prime motivating factor for the project as a way to improve children's achievement in basic skills (i.e., reading and math), the proposal and contract anticipated having a full curriculum at Banneker. For a variety of reasons, it took a good part of the first year of the program to get the complete curriculum "phased in." This led to problems, not only with the state and the

Union, but eventually with the community as well. The problem of the narrow curriculum at the beginning was compounded by what was referred to as the "top-out" problem. The top-out problem existed for those children who were able to work through the programmed materials provided in the beginning. When they had completed the sequence, it was discovered that they had "nowhere to go."

In February, Sandra Irons said:

> They're teaching reading and math, all day long! They keep saying the materials are coming, they're being developed, they're on the way. They have a group of children over there, about 45, who have tested completely out of the program. They have nothing for them to do.[22]

A Banneker teacher put the problem this way:

> When BRL came in in August, all they had for us was the Sullivan materials in reading and math. *That's all, nothing else.* So we started science in January, and we started social studies later than that. In math, we got our supplementary materials in March. And in reading the same thing, maybe a little earlier. These people came in there and did not have a program. And they're still working. This summer we're going to work on the course of study; we're still not together. No program for top-outs. And this was part of the problem. The Sullivan materials in reading and math are not entities in themselves; they have to be supplemented heavily. They do their things, but you have to work in other areas too.[23]

The problem of the narrow curriculum was easy prey for critics. This was made so by the fact that achievement test scores in reading and math were the things the company had guaranteed. Critics found it particularly easy to attack the company for teaching only reading and math when the company had guaranteed only reading and math. The fact that the proposal and the contract called for a broad curriculum and the public was assured that the intention was, and always had been, to have a broad curriculum, failed to still critics.

Gordon McAndrew saw the narrow beginning curriculum as a major difficulty with the program in its early stages. He looked back from January:

> Now I think one of the shortcomings, if you look back over the first six months, is that these other programs have not been phased in fast enough, in fact they're still not all phased in. Social studies came in in the fall, but not completely; science is just really starting now. And the enrichment is just getting phased in. As a result of some bugs that developed, we met quite a bit over Christmas. And that was one of my criticisms. And on the basis of my look at the thing, I had five points that I asked for from the staff, and we got those worked out, and those are in the process of being implemented during this month. My target is that by the end of January, all of the phases will begin. I don't really expect that until next fall that the complete kind of sophisticated bag, with the instructional objectives, clearly delineated and all that, I think it'll be until then before the thing is really in the kind of shape I'd like to see it.[24]

In the beginning of the project, the implications were strong that BRL was in possession of a complete system which they were going to demonstrate and which they had enough confidence in to guarantee its results. As problems arose, it became increasingly clear that the system was to be, in large part, developed on site.

Leadership Problems

Gordon McAndrew described the leadership problem in May:

> I think that one of the things the staff has probably been frustrated by, which has come out in various

meetings I've had with them is 'Who's the chief?' We're used to having somebody called the principal, even if he's kind of bad, we know who's the chief. Now, who is it here? Is it Kendrick? Was it June Gordon, when she was here? Is it Helen Mooney? Or is it Benford? Now we've got a guy named Fitch coming in—now who's he? I talked to Stern and Kendrick about these things—who the hell are all these people you have here? As you begin to try to describe it in retrospect, first there was Kendrick, and then Kendrick brought in somebody named Gordon, in addition to which there were a lot of people coming in and out, you know, consultants. Well, I would see the people coming in and out, and I'd say, well, here's somebody who's only going to be here a few weeks to work on this problem with these people. But there are a few people who have kind of stayed on through it. And, I think there has been a little bit of uncertainty in everybody's mind as to who they were and what their roles were. Now again, some of that I think is the process of discovery. You say, well I kind of got an idea that this person might come in and do generally this kind of thing—and when that person comes in his job becomes defined by his way of operating, and so forth. But that's OK with me; but the thing is, if I were a curriculum manager there, I'd kind of wonder; because then you have George Stern kind of coming in. On our side, it's a little clearer; but then there's Benford—what does he do? And then I came in and out more than I would in a normal school, and they could say, now why is he here like this? If I'm a teacher and if I have a kid who's giving me the fits, or if I have a problem about materials, where do I go? That ought to be and will have to be a little more sharply defined in the fall, even though it might continue to alter. I hope that at the end of the contract period, we'll be able to say we've had various kinds of relationships, but here's the way the administrative leadership of this kind of an enterprise ought to be.[25]

Part of the problem was "too many cooks," but part of the problem was the leadership style chosen by BRL. Don Kendrick, in talking about the company's ability to change things in order to assure the best use of their materials, revealed an attitude about change in an educational organization that pointed up his lack of experience with schools and teachers.

> That's one of the things we can do here. We change schedules. We're working on schedules right now to implement activities in the afternoons. You can do things like that, you can change the schedule, just say, we're not going to do that anymore, we're going to change. O.K., everybody, let's follow the leader, change it like this.[26]

Anyone with very much experience with change or with school people will recognize that change in schools is not so simple a thing as to be accomplished merely by saying, "O.K., everybody, let's follow the leader, change it like this." With Kendrick's aggressive style and inexperience with school people, and Benford's mild manner and unfamiliarity with BRL and their program, the authority division between the two men had to be something of a problem.

A top member of the School City staff recognized that, at least in part, the charges made by some teachers and aides that Kendrick was a dictator, were due to his style and to what teachers and aides perceived as an unresponsiveness on his part.

Otha Porter spoke of this leadership problem in December:

> All right, now you said something about the relationship of Kendrick and Benford, now let's talk about personalities as a human problem. Here I am, I've been a school principal for thirteen years. As a school principal I am king of all I survey, in terms of school property in my area. When School City or any one else signs a contract or an agreement with a company, and we're talking about funds, profit and loss, and that kind of business, you have to give the company representative certain leeway less the contract is no longer valid. Consequently, the principal, or the former principal must

assume an entirely new role. He assumes a role, say, of an assistant principal, in a sense, in terms of actual performance in a school. Then, when you kick in this business of money where people might be up tight in terms of the progress of the pupil, and you're talking about millions of dollars now, you have to be even more careful about how you operate the relationship you have with the company person in that particular case. The agreement is with the company.[27]

In Porter's mind, in December, 1970, Donald Kendrick was in charge.

Clarence Benford was well aware that the authority belonged to Kendrick. Earlier in February, he said ". . . being kept in the dark, expecting to know, but I don't know what for four years would be intolerable." He went on to say that if School City were to say in four years, "Clarence, you're at the helm, you run the ship," he'd have to answer, "I can't run the ship; I don't know where the controls are."[28]

This problem was not lost on the teachers. The experience-authority problems were illustrated by one teacher in relating the development of the report cards.

We had to go through several different report cards and he (Kendrick) never really got one because he never asked teachers. He trusted himself to come up with something out of this world; and he kept compounding mistakes like this.[29]

This is not to demean Donald Kendrick, who is a bright and hard-working individual, but is only to point out the difficulty of working in schools without an understanding of the culture of the school. One must expect different decisions to spring from different bases. Likewise, one must expect different reactions from different bases. A school principal, as supervisor in a General Motors' factory would get a different reaction to his directives and decisions, because of the nature of that particular work culture, than would a G.M. foreman who was familiar with the car manufacturing milieu. It therefore, is not surprising that teachers would react differently to a supervisor from industry than to a supervisor who was totally familiar with the nuances of education.

Some teachers thought Clarence Benford should have reacted to the problem differently, as well. Some said they thought Benford should have put "his job on the line" early in the project.

That the problem was a sensitive and difficult problem for School City was evidenced in a December, 1970, interview with School City central staff members, Otha Porter, Nicholas McDonald, and William Wallace, when a question was asked regarding the division of authority between School City's man and BRL's man at Banneker. The question elicited what the author could only describe as a tirade from Otha Porter. He asserted that anything the interviewers were to print had to be okayed by him first, and that "whatever information you have on that tape is confidential information." During this soliloquy, a particularly revealing thing was said: "When you put it on tape, it means we're not in a position to refute anything we might say."[30]

It should be pointed out, however, that when that particular sensitive nerve had recovered from its shock, Dr. Porter again became amenable and cooperative, and spoke about the relationship between BRL's man and School City's man, not exercising the censorship that he had threatened. The point is only that the problem was most sensitive and that School City, understandably, was extremely reluctant, at that time, to let the public know that there were any critical problems associated with the program.

The fact that Kendrick was in charge was to provide an issue the State used in attacking the program.

> The State Board was informed that the assigned principal of Banneker School does not regularly perform any of the functions ordinarily expected of the principal of an elementary school as specified by the *Administrative Handbook* on pages 165 through 168. The BRL center manager, who does not hold an Indiana certification of any kind, performs all of the principal's functions and is recognized as doing so by the Banneker staff.[31]

The conflict that developed between those involved in the

project and the state department of education is explored in Chapter Four.

The authority situation was to change with School City taking more control of the day to day situation and BRL beginning to concentrate more strongly on the developmental aspects of the program. This phenomenon is discussed more thoroughly in Chapter Five.

The project did develop problems and difficulties; however, major adjustments were to be made and the project was to survive at least the first year. Nevertheless, Charles Smith's remarks made in December, 1970, were to prove prophetic.

> I think the BRL school as presently run is a badly administered school. I would question, at this point, whether they can even teach for those rather specific skills that are written out in the guarantee. If I had to make a prediction right now, I would predict BRL would not be here for the duration of their 4-year contract unless they change the system and they change the administration of the school.[32]

---

[1] Stated by Gordon McAndrew, Superintendent, School City of Gary, in an interview with the author in January, 1971.

[2] Contract between BRL and School City of Gary, pp. 2-4.

[3] Stated by Ira Judge in an interview with the author, in May, 1971.

[4] BRL Proposal for Right to Learn Project, p. 11.

[5] BRL-School City Contract.

[6] BRL Proposal . . . , *op. cit.,* p. 16.

[7] McAndrew interview, January, 1971, *op. cit.*

[8] Stated by Otha Porter, Assistant to the Superintendent, School City of Gary, in an interview with the author in January, 1971.

[9] Moscove, Francine, *The Experiment at Banneker School,* Writer's Workshop Pamphlet No. 3, May, 1971, p. 6.

[10] Stated by Donald Kendrick in an interview conducted by Minnie Perrin Berson, in *Journal of the Association of Childhood Education,* March, 1971.

[11] *Ibid.*

57

[12]*Ibid.*

[13]Stated by Raymond V. Komenich, Director of Personnel, School City of Gary, in a letter to Charles O. Smith, President of Gary Teachers' Union, October 2, 1970.

[14]McAndrew interview, May, 1971, *op. cit.*

[15]Stated by Charles Smith, President, Gary Teachers' Union, in an interview with the author in February, 1971.

[16]Komenich letter, October, 1970, *op. cit.*

[17]Judge interview, May, 1971, *op. cit.*

[18]McAndrew interview, January, 1971, *op. cit.*

[19]Komenich letter, October, 1970, *op. cit.*

[20]Porter interview, January, 1971, *op. cit.*

[21]Irons, Sandra, Address at Truth and Soul in Teaching Conference of the AFT, Chicago, Illinois, January 16, 1971.

[22]*Ibid.*

[23]Judge interview, May, 1971, *op. cit.*

[24]McAndrew interview, January, 1971, *op. cit.*

[25]McAndrew interview, May, 1971, *op. cit.*

[26]Stated by Donald Kendrick in an interview with Orest Ochitwa in October, 1970.

[27]Porter interview, December, 1970, *op. cit.*

[28]Stated by Clarence Benford in an interview with the author in December, 1970.

[29]Judge interview, May, 1971, *op. cit.*

[30]Porter interview, December, 1970, *op. cit.*

[31]Indiana State Board of Education, *Minutes of Meeting,* January 19, 1071, p. 2.

[32]Stated by Charles Smith in an interview with the author in December, 1970.

FOUR

OUTSIDE CHALLENGES TO THE PROJECT

With all the internal problems of the project to try to adjust for, School City and BRL had to face intense challenges from outside the project. A line from the Merle Travis song, *Sixteen Tons,* comes to mind; "One fist of iron, the other of steel, if the right one don't-a get you, then the left one will." One could say that this chapter deals with the "left one."

The challenges offered by the Gary Teachers' Union and the Office of the State Superintendent of Public Instruction are inextricably intertwined both with one another and with the internal problems of the project.

While the resulting conflicts were fought on the grounds of law, rule, and regulation, the reasons the conflict was joined by the various parties is perhaps more complex, important, and illuminating.

Union Misgivings

In January, 1971, Otha Porter put his finger on a most significant problem:

> The unique thing about this program they're telling us that 'we can improve the quality of instruction at no additional cost.' So when a school system says, can we afford BRL? the answer is yes, because it doesn't cost you any more. Now that's a big point. You see many of these other programs that you have around the country that you've read about keep the regular staff and the

program is more or less an add-on, which really isn't that much of a change; consequently, you don't have any problems with the teachers' union because they're always happy if you add-on. When you talk about replacement, no one is happy.[1]

The promise that a program will change things drastically is hard to take for those whose ego is invested in the status quo. This weakness in human personality makes success of any program almost impossible to achieve, let alone to live with gracefully. Porter pointed this out in March;

One of the problems we're faced with in the education community—not only with our program, but with other programs—is, it might work. Now that's a big problem. Because if we are successful in these programs around the country, it's going to shake up a lot of things.[2]

The "replacement" that Porter says no one would be happy about is primarily the replacement of certificated teachers with paraprofessionals and materials-based instruction. This is automatically offensive to a teachers' Union.

McAndrew testified before the U.S. Senate Select Committee on Equal Educational Opportunity that "We had thought it sacred that there be one teacher for every thirty pupils." He went on to point out that the project showed "there is nothing magic about it." McAndrew told the committee that the "adult"/pupil ratio is more important than the "teacher"/pupil ratio.[3]

If that can be shown to be true, and if the system that makes such changes apparently does indeed do a better job with no increased costs, then the teachers' union simply has no choice but to attack such a program with their best shots. To do less would cost too high a price with their membership, particularly during times when the teacher "shortage" has turned into a teacher "surplus."

The changes proposed and implemented were not the only things to stick in the craw of the Union. The manner in which the change was instituted seemed to many observers to say the least, somewhat cavalier.

Efram Sigel, in the book, *Accountability and the Controversial Role of the Performance Contractors,* in talking of the problems with the Gary contract, said:

> Another problem with the project—the most serious one—is its political implications. No teachers' union could read the Gary contract without misgivings. While the agreement specifically requires BRL to comply with all applicable laws, ordinances and codes of state and local governments, it says nothing specific about observing the contractual obligation of the board vis-a-vis teachers.

> To an extent, BRL hopes to counter the opposition from the teachers' union by developing a constituency in the local community, and among the teachers at Banneker. The company was one of the first to realize the potency—and the potential—of the drive for community control of urban schools. Part of its marketing strategy for Project Read is to champion the cause of 'disenfranchised' parents who have no say in the educational programs that affect their children.

> Employing parents of Banneker children as paraprofessionals obviously plays a role in this strategy, as do the hefty overtime checks for teachers at the school.[4]

Sigel went on to point out that "In the long run, however, no one—and especially not a company—can win at pitting community groups against teachers' unions."[5]

History of the Union Conflict

In a lengthy press release called *Education vs. Business,* the Gary Teachers' Union recounted that:

BANNEKER

Gary's 'contracted Curriculum Center' became known to the Gary Teachers' Union, Local No. 4, AFT, in the spring of 1970, in a lengthy booklet called THE RIGHT TO LEARN. At that time, we were informed that it would be looked into and possibly started in the fall of 1971.

We heard about it again on July 14, 1970, at a school board meeting, and the superintendent quoted: 'It would take extensive negotiations with the Union and the State Department of Public Instruction for the successful execution of the program'.[6]

The press release went on to say that:

On August 27, 1970, at a board meeting, members of the Union pointed out the errors and flaws in performance contracting—the reduction of the number of licensed teachers, the involuntary transfers, class size, the single salary schedule, and the 15-day transfer notice.[7]

It was during this meeting that Board President Holliday made an offer to the Union to contract for a school on a performance basis. McAndrew remembered the Board's feelings at that point as "We appreciate your criticisms, now what we'd like you to do is instead of telling us what's wrong with this, we'd like you to develop a proposal which you think makes sense." McAndrew said that that's never been done and moreover the union had never come to the Board with educational proposals, "only bread and butter issues."[8]

Smith deemed the offer unworthy of reply and went on to point out that the Union had no materials to advertise and that, in any case, the Union didn't think enough of the quality of the Banneker project to care to "compete with BRL on BRL's terms."[9]

Sandra Irons of the Gary Teachers' Union, said that during the following school board meeting one of the board members ". . . informed the GTU they were going to file lawsuits because we were charging them with collusion or what have you."[10]

Though that threat was never carried out, the fact that it was even made is an indication that the board and the Union were finding communication between them to be more strained.

In October, 1970, the Union threatened to strike over alleged violation to their contract with School City. McAndrew responded that the Union had failed to use the grievance procedure spelled out in their contract. The Board and the Superintendent also indicated they would listen to an advisory arbiter. The result was that the Union stalled the strike and filed a grievance on October 21, 1970.

The grievance asserted that:

> The School City of Gary has reduced the number of teachers at the Banneker Elementary School below the number which is required under the terms of the 1970-1971 Agreement between the Gary Board of School Trustees and the Gary Teachers' Union, Local No. 4, AFT. This reduction in the number of licensed teachers assigned to the Banneker School, the involuntary transfer of teachers which was occasioned by that staff reduction and the consequent increase in class size violate provisions of the Agreement.[11]

The grievance report went on to detail the violations mentioned, pointing out which sections of the Agreement were violated. The report also called into issue the method of selection of those teachers declared surplus and the method used to later add teachers to the Banneker staff. The Agreement indicated that staff may only be transferred on a seniority basis of last-in—first-out and further that, when additions to the staff become necessary, those teachers previously transferred must be given first choice to return.

In addition, the report questioned the "approval of a clause in the contract with a private consultant firm under the terms of which the School City agrees to transfer teachers upon fifteen (15) days notice by the private consultant."[12]

BANNEKER

McAndrew called the conference required in the grievances procedure, and Union and administration representatives met on October 28, 1970.

Ernie Hernandez, writing for the *Gary Post-Tribune,* reported that ". . . nothing positive was accomplished, both told the reporter. But they noted they chalked off another required step toward solution of the Union/administration dispute."[13]

McAndrew later answered the charges in writing, again as called for in the grievances procedure, asking the Union to "give the Banneker program a chance."[14]

Arbitration

McAndrew's answer to the charges failed to satisfy the Union, and in December, an arbiter was chosen from a panel of nine candidates presented by the American Arbitration Association (AAA). The procedure called for School City and the GTU to each rank the nine candidates in order of preference. The AAA was then to add the scores and select the candidate with the lowest score.

This procedure resulted in the selection of John F. Stembower, a Chicago attorney and law professor. Stembower was GTU's first choice and the sixth choice of School City. The Board viewed the selection of their sixth choice as unfair and refused to participate further in the proceedings.

AAA rejected the Board's protest and it was reported in the *Gary Post-Tribune* that ". . . Allen K. Miller, co-director of AAA, said he could not deviate from the established procedure. In forty-five years of administering labor-management arbitrations, the AAA has never had such an objection, he said."[15]

The AAA scheduled a hearing for January 20, 1971. Union representatives were present but no School City representatives showed up. Stembower could have proceeded with the session hearing evidence from the Union and making an "ex-parte" finding, but the union asked for a continuance. Stembower reset the hearing for January 25, 1971.

Again the board failed to show, and Stembower did hear evidence presented by the Union.

OUTSIDE CHALLENGES TO THE PROJECT

On February 17, 1971, Stembower ruled that the Gary School Board had violated the terms of its agreement with the Union and called for immediate reinstatement of the transferred teachers.

Response to the Arbitration

Ernie Hernandez reported that ". . . the Gary Teachers' Union is finding out that an arbitrator's decision is hardly enough to turn things around at the controversial Banneker School."[16]

The fact that there was no legal provision for the Union to sue, the Board relegated the Union to only the use of public opinion to try to get the Board to abide by the arbitrator's findings. The question of binding arbitration was the subject of a law suit that was not to be settled during the first year of the performance contract at Banneker.

In addition to the fact that the findings were only "advisory," the Office of the State Superintendent of Public Instruction was, at about that same time, engaged in action with School City on certain questions, some of which overlapped the objections raised by the Union.

The OSPI action involved the decommissioning of Banneker which could have cost School City nearly $200,000 in state aid. The response on School City's part to the challenge by OSPI was understandably more vigorous than their response to the Union challenge.

Hernandez reported that ". . . while Gary School City President Gordon McAndrew is taking steps to restore Banneker to its licensed status, nothing is being done to comply with the decision rendered by the arbiter, John F. Stembower."[17]

Charles Smith said about the arbiter's decision that "we've said all along that it would be a better program if they simply abided by the Union agreement."[18]

Hernandez concluded the article in the *Post-Tribune,* dealing with the Stembower award, by suggesting that even if the Board eventually came around to abiding by the decision, that the ruling itself "can hardly be deemed a motivating factor. McAndrew and the Board can always say the charges were prompted by state regulations and the need for state commissioning, which is worth $200,000 of state money."[19]

Union Withdrawal

It appeared that when the Union leadership weighed the advisory nature of the arbitration, the difficulty with a suspicious black community that would be caused by a strike against a program "to help black kids learn better," and the overlapping nature of many of OSPI's objections, that they decided it would be wise to let the State carry the battle to School City.

McAndrew, in recounting the planning of the program, indicated his feeling that while more talk and negotiating with the Union might have helped, he was ". . . not sure it would have resolved the basic issues, because you'd still come to a point where you'd say this is the way we want to do it, and they'd say this is the way it has to be."[20] He went on further to suggest that he felt School City was "disposed to do it" and the union was "disposed against it." He didn't feel that the planning would have been "substantially changed if we had talked longer."[21]

The OSPI Challenge

After the early attempts to stop the project before it began failed [these attempts were described in Chapter Two], the Office of the State Superintendent of Public Instruction began an ongoing evaluation of the project. It is obvious that OSPI had neither the staff nor inclination to conduct a detailed ongoing evaluation of each of the approximately 2,200 elementary schools in Indiana. But the Banneker project was threatening, not only because it was different, but because it drew wide publicity, as well.

At the October meeting of the Commission on General Education of the State Board of Education, Superintendent Richard D. Wells suggested that OSPI provide staff members from the Divisions of Curriculum and School Finance to assist with the evaluation.[22]

OUTSIDE CHALLENGES TO THE PROJECT

Assistant Superintendent for Instructional Services, John S. Hand, and Director, Division of Curriculum, William B. Strange, later led teams of OSPI personnel on three visits to Banneker.

On October 20, 1970, a visit was made which, in addition to Hand and Strange, included a reading consultant, two psychological services consultants, and a school finance consultant.

The November 9 and 10, 1970, visit included consultants from the areas of reading, elementary education, social studies, psychological services, and the Assistant Director of the Curriculum Division.

The January 7, 1971, visit included consultants from the areas of reading, elementary education, social studies, and the Director of the Division of Inspection.[23]

When one recognizes that this many people made trips to Gary to look at one elementary school, one begins to see the seriousness with which OSPI viewed the challenge of the performance contracted project underway at Banneker.

The First Report

In a report to Superintendent Wells, dated November 18, 1970, John Hand described the October 20, 1970, and November 9 and 10, 1970, visits. This report was generally negative, spending much of its bulk comparing what was perceived by the investigators with what was promised in the proposal and contract. This might be a very necessary activity for someone to undertake, but it did point out that OSPI's interest in the project was far deeper than the enforcement of state rules and regulations.

Hand's November 18 report made it clear that the investigators felt from the beginning that they were not getting the full story from School City. The narrative of the report began with the statement that "A concerted effort was made by Otha Porter and the BRL staff members to shepherd the team, so that little contact would be made with teachers and students."[24]

Later in the same memorandum, Hand asserted that:

The School City does engage in a game of subterfuge

67

which required that communication between Banneker and the Administrative Center be through Clarence Benford, but Benford's function is limited to figurehead types of activities and formal responsibilities, such as signing requisitions *after* Kendrick has already signed and approved them.[25]

The charge that BRL is in "total control" is reiterated several times in that November 18 memo.

Hand also argued with BRL's claim that the program was individualized. He had asked Kendrick what was done for those children who ". . . do not find programmed instruction compatible with their learning style" and had received the response that it was a difficult problem. In the November 18 memo, ". . . difficult or not, a program that fails to make some such accommodation has no legitimate right to label itself an individualized program."[26] He went on to assert that the children are "all being run through the same instructional mould."[27]

It was interesting to note three things in the arguments over individualization. One was that the State had no rules and regulations that would be broken by an imperfect attempt at individualization. The second point was that the arguments used against the program were that the program didn't match up with what was promised, rather than that the program was contrary to rules or regulations (with respect to individualization). The third point was that in the normal Indiana elementary school, any arguments over individualization simply didn't come up, as the standard procedure was to take all students, convoy-like, through the same material at the same time.

It was only on page 6 of the memo that State Requirements were dealt with. Hand pointed out that the program "appears to be in possible violation" at four points. These areas included certification of administrator (Kendrick was not certifiable, but School City maintained that Benford was the building administrator), the use of materials not on the State adopted list, time allotment for the various subjects, and role differentiation between teachers and paraprofessionals. Though about the last area, he pointed out that ". . . there may not be any violation in this vagueness of role."[28]

The last point requires the comment that the role of the paraprofessional was not clearly defined by rules or regulations of OSPI or the State Board of Education.

In summary, the memo regarding the OSPI's first team visit served to illustrate that while the weapon available to OSPI for use against the project was rule and regulation, the concern of OSPI went far beyond the enforcement of stated laws, rules, and regulations. This broader concern, coupled with emotional and political mistrust of School City and the project served, in part, to explain the intense scrutiny of the project by the State.

This close observation by the State prompted Otha Porter to observe that:

> The same rules apply in Indianapolis, Evansville, in ghetto schools, and rural schools. You find ratios of 40 to 1 in ghetto schools, and schools in rural areas operating with half uncertified personnel. Some school systems don't bring their problems to anyone's attention because their superintendents are not go-getters. Talk about rocking the boat, they don't even have a boat to rock and the State commissions those schools.[29]

The Second Report

On January 11, 1971, John Hand prepared a report to the State Board of Education regarding the Banneker project. In addition to reasserting that "the Banneker School is a BRL operation; at the present time with BRL staff members making all administrative and instructional decisions," he reiterated the earlier concerns over state adopted textbooks, time apportionment, administration, and certification. In addition to those concerns, he raised issues regarding competitors bidding for the contractual furnishing of instructional materials and supplies, and the pupil/teacher ratio of the school.[30]

As in the earlier memo, the perceptions of the OSPI team were, in many cases, compared against the promise of the contract, as well as against State rule and regulation. In response to Banneker teachers and administrators' assertions that science and social

69

studies had not been "phased in" earlier because children who cannot read cannot successfully handle science and social studies. Hand wrote that ". . . if this is truly an individualized program, it seems strange that it cannot provide non-reading or slower reading children with appropriate materials so that their Science and Social Studies literacy will not be neglected."[31] Never mind that these "appropriate materials" are hardly common if they exist at all. The point here is that "individualized program" had different meanings to the parties involved in the conflict surrounding the project.

Hand was careful to protect the School City professional staff working at Banneker from his criticisms of the program. He said that ". . . our impression has been that they are dedicated professionals who are doing the best they can with a program that was imposed upon the school without their advice or consent."[32]

Whatever the validity (many were valid at the time) of the criticisms of the program, it was important to remember the vigor of the response to the challenge offered to the establishment by the outsider. The challenge by private industry was not limited to teachers and administrators in schools, but included the regulatory agency as well. One parent of a Banneker student was reported to have said that ". . . our children have been in the State approved program in the past and they haven't been too successful and we think we have to come up with something new."[33] One must expect that any different way of educating children will be met with resistance, not only by teachers that have ego investments in traditional ways, but by regulatory agencies as well.

A Warning

The project and the January 11, 1971, memorandum was the subject of a joint meeting of the three commissions of the Indiana State Board of Education on January 19, 1971. A contingent from Gary was present that included Assistant Superintendent Heron Battle, Otha Porter, and the Learning Director at Banneker, Clarence Benford. McAndrew was not present and that fact was cause for consternation by Wells and some members of the Board and OSPI staff. McAndrew's absence was to be strongly pointed out at a later meeting. His absence was viewed as not being properly respectful of the authority of the State Board.

Just as the meeting seemed, to the author, to be drifting toward the decommissioning of the School, Board member, Richard S. Barack, a junior high school principal in Gary, read a prepared statement in which he pled the case for the ". . . feeling and the educational well-being of the children at Banneker School."[34] He suggested to the Board that removing State aid from the school might be "compounding the problem" and made suggestions that Banneker be put on one month's warning status and that OSPI and the Board offer help to School City to bring the program to conformity with State law.

Barack concluded his statement by asserting that "at this point our decision should be based on not how this effects [sic] BRL or the Gary School Board or the Superintendent of Schools, but how it effects [sic] the basic education of seven hundred boys and girls."[35]

A motion to recommend to the General Commission that the Banneker School be decommissioned was defeated by an 8 to 6 vote. The full State Board could only advise the Commission on General Education of their feelings as the power to decommission resided in the General Commission.

A motion that essentially consisted of Barack's recommendation was made by another member of the Board, and was passed by a 13 to 1 vote.[36]

Hand's Report on Educational Quality

During the January 19 meeting, Hand expressed reservations about the quality of the educational program at Banneker, and he submitted another memorandum to the State Board dated February 12, 1971, detailing those reservations. Even though changes had been made in an attempt to more closely conform to the rules and regulations, the February 12 memorandum was written in a much more caustic style than Hand's preceding memorandum to the State Board.

Hand claimed this assessment to be from two perspectives: ". . . the promise and performance of the contractual relationship as it relates to educational quality and additional specific observations not directly related to the contract."[37]

Hand pointed out that since he had not visited Banneker before the project began, he could not compare the program to any previous program at Banneker. He did not point out that there were many programs in operation in Gary and other cities in Indiana that closely paralleled the rather traditional program offered at Banneker in previous years.

In his assessment of educational quality, Hand had requested the curriculum design from School City. After he received a "voluminous packet of materials" he complained that they not only appeared to have been "hastily assembled" but that they were "not bound," had no title page or introductory statement," and that "in addition, there were serious grammatical and usage errors in the narrative portions of the document, fragmented sentences, and sentences that made no sense."[38]

Hand also pointed out that the contract contained a statement that ". . . respect for the change of institutions by lawful means" shall be taught and commented that "the flagrant disregard BRL and the School City of Gary have shown toward State Rules and Regulations during the first four months of the operation of this program raises an interesting question about the credibility of this contractual item."[39]

Hand capped this very negative document with the conclusion that:

1. The Banneker program is *not* a well-rounded instructional program.

2. BRL has *not* succeeded in fulfilling a sizeable number of its contractual obligations.

3. The Banneker program is *not* what the contract purports it to be.

4. There is nothing uniquely innovative about the Banneker program except (a) the abdication of professional responsibility on the part of the School City of Gary, and

5. The placement of the primary emphasis upon building and maintaining a systems model instead of upon the children and their needs and interests.[40] [emphasis his]

In a memorandum to the Commission on General Education dated just five days later, on February 18, 1971, Hand took an almost conciliatory stance in comparison to the earlier memo to the State Board. He pointed out changes that had occurred in the Banneker program to bring it toward conformity with the law, in addition to pointing out areas still requiring correction.

The summary of this short (three pages) document was interesting to compare to the conclusions he drew just five days previously.

During the past month, a concerted effort has been made at Banneker School to comply with State requirements. Discrepancies still exist, however, in the use of State-adopted textbooks, in administration, and in the pupil-teacher ratio.[41]

One could only guess at what might have prompted the apparent change of attitude toward Banneker that Hand exhibited.

Decommissioning

On February 18, the State Board of Education again held a meeting concerning the Banneker problem. Again, in addition to OSPI staff and the State Board, the contingent from Gary was led by Dr. Battle and was notable because it again failed to contain Dr. McAndrew. That fact served to arouse the State Board to the extent that the minutes of that meeting show that one of two basic questions concerning the Board at that meeting, was the question: "Why the Superintendent from the Gary Public Schools never appeared at the State Board meetings?"[42]

McAndrew must have known that his failure to appear before the Board had to anger Wells and some of the Board members. Part of that response probably had to do with a personal animosity between Wells and McAndrew. McAndrew said once in discussing the State confrontation that "I wouldn't have responded as I did if Dick Wells had not been in that seat."[43]

After declaring that ". . . any change for the better should be approved" and "the best ways of education should be found and encouraged, the Board voted to:

> Recommend to the General Commission that the Gary School Board of Trustees and the Gary School Superintendent be notified they have not fully conformed to the rules and regulations of the State Board of Education and the Banneker School is to be decommissioned as a result of these violations, effective immediately.[44]

Richard Barack, the Board member from Gary, abstained. The General Commission acted on the recommendation later the same day.

Public Reaction to Decommissioning

The action to decommission the school, and McAndrew's immediate reaction, received wide publicity in the press. In an article entitled "Banneker Cut-off Effects 'Nothing'—McAndrew" appearing in the *Gary Post-Tribune* on February 19, 1971, McAndrew stated that the school "should and could be properly commissioned when the commission meets again March 4."[45]

The Associated Press reported McAndrew as saying, "I hope we don't get so involved in nitpicking that we forget schools are there to help children."[46]

The Indianapolis Star reported on February 20, 1971, in a story headlined, "Whitcomb Asks Study of Gary School Ban," that "The Governor said it is possible he may ask the commission to reconsider its action."[47] That story also reported that a member of the House Education Committee, Robert L. Jones, Jr., blamed the school's difficulties on the "National Education Association, bulwark of traditional education." Jones was reported to have said, "They're just trying to discredit it, they're scared to death of it."[48]

In an editorial broadcast at various times on February 24 and 25, 1971, the Chicago television station, WMAQ-TV, took a broadside at the Board's action, saying, "The State Board objected to the experiment because it was different . . ." and "tradition struck a blow at progress."[49]

OSPI and School City After Decommissioning

On February 19, 1971, John Hand wrote a letter to Gordon McAndrew, officially informing him of the action of the Commission on General Education, acknowledging the efforts of School City to bring the project into conformity with state rules and regulations and pointing out the areas in which improvement was required.

The areas in dispute had diminished to only the use of state-adopted texts, pupil/teacher ratio, and the continuing concern over the administration of the program.

School City had already begun the process of requesting waivers from the Commission on Textbook Adoption and the pupil/teacher ratio seemed to merely require clarification, but Hand asked questions about the ". . . principal's present role and how it related to the role of the center manager in regard to . . ." seven specific functions.[50]

McAndrew answered Hand's letter of February 19, 1971, with a letter dated February 26, 1971. McAndrew responded that the waiver requests for textbooks were in process, the teacher/pupil ratio was within prescribed limits (he attached a list of the teachers at Banneker) and enclosed a letter written to Otha Porter by Clarence Benford. In Benford's letter to Porter, he not only responded to each of Hand's seven questions, but took the ". . . opportunity to state clearly to you and all concerned that, I am the Principal of Banneker School and exercise all the authority and responsibilities the position of Principal implies."[51]

As Hall and Rapp pointed out in their Rand report, by spring of 1971 ". . . both in public announcements and in actual fact the direct cognizance, control, and responsibility of School City was clearly established. The authority of McAndrew, Battle, Porter, and Benford over the program was no longer in doubt."[52]

The changes in administration had begun with a December visit to Banneker by McAndrew and had become obvious by early spring.

The Recommissioning

The author remembers the March 10, 1971, meeting of the Commission on General Education that was to decide on the possible recommissioning of Banneker, as being charged with emotion.

This meeting was to be the last meeting of the General Commission to be chaired by Richard D. Wells. Wells had lost his re-election bid to John J. Loughlin who was to take over as State Superintendent on the following Monday. McAndrew later said about his relationship with Loughlin that "I know full well that if Loughlin and his people had been in at the time we went through this, that the whole State issue would never have arisen."[53]

Whether McAndrew's assessment of Loughlin's feelings was accurate is not the point; the point is that McAndrew, and many others, for that matter, were sure that if Banneker was not recommissioned by the Wells administration, that it surely would be recommissioned when Loughlin and his people took over the next week.

This may help explain the seemingly cavalier attitude that McAndrew sometimes exhibited toward Wells and the Commission.

An article that appeared in the March 15, 1971, issue of *Newsweek,* and which came to Wells' attention just before the March 10 meeting, and which he mentioned several times there, did nothing to calm the situation. In that article, "Gary officials" in commenting on the decommissioning, were reported to have noted that "there has never been any love lost between the small-town politicians who dominate the state government and increasingly black-dominated Gary," and it appeared that the decommissioning was "a capricious swan song by state school superintendent Richard D. Wells, who has a reputation for arbitrary actions."[54]

To say that Wells was incensed as he opened the meeting would be an understatement.

The Gary contingent to the March 10 meeting, was led, at least, by Dr. McAndrew, and included, in addition to other School City staff members, George Stern, President of BRL.

Wells read a short statement at the opening of the meeting, then spent several minutes berating McAndrew and Stern. During this time, Wells brought up such things as the *Newsweek* article and the previous absence at meetings of McAndrew and Stern. George Stern sat silent during the meeting, and the author remembers McAndrew as parrying only the deepest Wells' thrusts.

McAndrew then read a short statement in support of the recommissioning, and Gary staff members answered many questions from Wells and the Commission members.

At one point, when asked what were to be the arrangements for reimbursement for those sixth grade students that failed to show month for month gains in reading and math at the end of the first year, Dr. Robert Shearer, Assistant Superintendent for Finance for School City, produced a memorandum of agreement signed by McAndrew and Stern dated March 9, 1971. Shearer didn't point out that McAndrew and Stern had produced that memorandum on the day before the Board meeting.

As the mood of the Commission seemed, to the author, to be turning against the recommissioning, Richard Barack, of the Commission and Gary, called for a lunch recess.

Barack later explained that he pointed out to Wells and the rest of the Commission that Loughlin was reported to be in favor of the experiment, and with public pressure for the experiment, Banneker would surely be recommissioned by the succeeding administration. He pointed out the image of the Commission would be more enhanced by its recommissioning it than by denying it.[55]

Barack later said that the Governor had not influenced the recommissioning, though McAndrew was reported to think he had,[56] but that the move was made by the Commission.

When the Commission returned from the lunch break, Dr. Reber moved for recommissioning and the motion was passed unanimously. The recommissioning was made "provisional" though this was probably a face-saving device, as evidenced by the fact that no one from OSPI returned to Banneker for the duration of the first year.

McAndrew later assessed the conflict with OSPI by suggesting that the "State's pressuring" caused no change in direction in Banneker, that all the changes that were made, BRL and School City had intended to make before the state raised the issues. McAndrew did, however, admit that perhaps the "pressuring" may have brought about a change in "timing."[57]

Stern assessed the outside challenges to the project in the May issue of *School Management:*

> The union and later the State Department of Education would have taken the guts out of the program and invalidated the entire thing. What they wanted to do was to achieve the objectives without making any changes. It would have been the old system again and it would have had as much of a chance to succeed as the old system had, which was not much.[58]

---

[1] Stated by Otha Porter, Assistant to the Superintendent, School City of Gary, in an interview with the author in January, 1971.

[2] Stated by Otha Porter, Assistant to the Superintendent, School City of Gary, in an interview with the author in March, 1971.

[3] Zuckerman, Ed, "Banneker 'Report Card' in Works," *Gary-Post Tribune,* September 15, 1971, p. B-1.

[4] Sigel, Efram, and Sobel, Myra, *Accountability and the Controversial Role of the Performance Contractors,* p. 31.

[5] *Ibid.*

[6] Gary Teachers' Union, Local No. 4, AFT-CIO, *Education vs. Business,* Press release, November, 1971, p. 1.

[7] *Ibid.,* p. 2.

[8] Irons, Sandra, Address at Truth and Soul in Teaching Conference of the AFT, Chicago, January 16, 1971.

[9] Stated by Gordon McAndrew, Superintendent, School City of Gary, in an interview with the author in January, 1971.

[10] Stated by Charles Smith, President, Gary Teachers' Union, in an interview with the author in February, 1971.

[11] Gary Teachers' Union No. 1-70, *Grievance Report,* October 21, 1970.

[12] *Ibid.*

[13] Hernandez, Ernie, "McAndrew, Union Meet on Grievance," *Gary Post-Tribune,* October 29, 1970, p. A-8.

[14] Stated by Gordon McAndrew in a letter to Charles O. Smith, November 3, 1970.

[15] Hernandez, Ernie, "Arbitration on Banneker is Continued," *Gary Post-Tribune,* January 21, 1971, p. B-2.

[16] *Ibid.*

[17] *Ibid.*

[18] *Ibid.*

[19] *Ibid.*

[20] Stated by Gordon McAndrew, Superintendent, School City of Gary, in an interview with the author in May, 1971.

[21] *Ibid.*

[22] *Minutes of the Meeting of the Commission on General Education,* Indiana State Board of Education, October 15, 1970.

[23] Stated by John S. Hand, in a letter to the State Board of Education, January 11, 1971.

[24] Hand, J. S., Indiana Assistant Superintendent for Instructional Services, *Memorandum to Superintendent Wells,* November 18, 1970.

[25] *Ibid.*

[26] *Ibid.*

[27] *Ibid.*

[28] *Ibid.*

[29] Stated by Otha Porter, Assistant to the Superintendent, School City of Gary, in an interview with the author in February, 1971.

[30] Hand memorandum, January 11, 1971, *op. cit.*

[31] *Ibid.*

[32] *Ibid.*

[33] Porter interview, February, 1971, *op. cit.*

BANNEKER

[34] From a statement read to the State Board of Education during the Banneker School Hearing, January 19, 1971.

[35] *Ibid.*

[36] Minutes of the meeting of the Indiana State Board of Education, January 19, 1971.

[37] Hand, J. S., Memorandum to the State Board of Education, February 12, 1971.

[38] *Ibid.*

[39] *Ibid.*

[40] *Ibid.*

[41] Hand, J. S., Memorandum to the Commission on General Education, February 17, 1971.

[42] Minutes of the Meeting of the Indiana State Board of Education, February 18, 1971.

[43] McAndrew interview, May, 1971, *op. cit.*

[44] Minutes of meeting . . ., February 18, *op. cit.*

[45] "Banneker Cut-off Effects 'Nothing'—McAndrew," *Gary Post-Tribune,* February 19, 1971, p. B-1.

[46] "Experimental School Aid Halted," Associated Press Release, February 19, 1971.

[47] "Whitcomb Asks Study of School Ban," *The Indianapolis Star,* February 20, 1971, p. A-4.

[48] *Ibid.*

[49] Editorial broadcast by WMAQ-TV at various times on February 24-25, 1971.

[50] Hand, J. S., Letter to Gordon L. McAndrew, February 19, 1971.

[51] Benford, C. L., Letter to Otha L. Porter, February 5, 1971.

[52] Rand report, *op. cit.,* p. 30.

[53] McAndrew interview, May, 1971, *op. cit.*

[54] "Banneker at Bay," *Newsweek,* March 15, 1971, p. 95.

[55] Stated by Richard S. Barack, in a conversation with the author in September, 1972.

[56] "Stockton and Gary Portray Two Views on Contracting," *Education Daily,* April 1, 1971.

[57] McAndrew interview, May, 1971, *op. cit.*

[58] Cray, D. C., "What's Happening in Gary?" *School Management,* May, 1971, p. 24.

FIVE

THE END OF THE BEGINNING

The internal problems with the Banneker project had become so intense during December, 1970, that one School City administrator, in looking back over that time, said ". . . if it had not been for Christmas vacation, there would be no Banneker."

Ernie Hernandez, reporting in the December 20, 1970, issue of the *Gary Post-Tribune,* wrote:

> During the past week the aides, called 'learning supervisors,' threatened a strike or a mass resignation as they complained that the director of the center, Don Kendricks [sic], has acted like a dictator by issuing orders without consulting the persons affected.[1]

Hernandez also reported that ". . . 11 of the 22 (teachers) had formally or informally asked for transfers or had plans of dropping out of Banneker."[2]

A Banneker teacher, in discussing the December problems, said:

> (Kendrick) would try to tell me something reasonable; and then he'd talk to somebody else and try to tell them something that would please them. Of course you do that and you don't have the ability to come through, you're going to get caught up. This is what happened in December.[3]

The intense internal pressures prompted McAndrew to hold several meetings with the Banneker staff over the Christmas vacation. During these meetings, the curriculum managers began to acquire more authority and to take more responsibility for the success of the program, until, as Hall and Rapp stated in the Rand report, ". . . by the end of the year, teachers were exercising a strong voice and considerable authority over the program through the Curriculum Managers Committee."[4]

At this time, when internal pressures were causing McAndrew and the School City staff to begin exercising more control over the project, it needs to be remembered that OSPI was providing plenty of external pressure on School City to take over the full administration of the project. At one point, in January, a School City administrator remarked that Kendrick's role had been reduced to that of a "mighty powerful consultant."

A Banneker teacher looked at the changes that began to affect the program after Christmas vacation meetings and said:

> Ever since January—and these changes didn't happen fast; there were pressures and counter pressures, they would send experts in—honest-to-God, now, they would send in experts from their company who were company people who couldn't make any recommendations or do a damned thing.[5]

But, as George Stern pointed out in the May issue of *School Management,* "what BRL can do, is to get things done rapidly, differently, and effectively, to evaluate unfavorable situations and to correct them in a hurry."[6] Stern got an evaluation of an "unfavorable situation" in that first December and set about correcting it.

Correcting the Unfavorable Situation

As one BRL employee stationed at Banneker remembers it, "George kept coming around saying 'we've got to individualize.' We thought 'what is that man talking about?' We were working so hard—what does he expect us to do? We just didn't know. They finally had to go to the outside."[7]

School City had to go outside, for BRL, to attempt to find a solution to their problem. Then BRL was forced to find an educator to bring in, in order to help solve the problems that had developed within the project. A BRL employee remembers that they found Dr. Brian Fitch in the Upper Midwest Regional Educational Laboratory in Minneapolis. In talking with Fitch, they thought they had found someone who could help solve the problem of individualization. Fitch had been working with individualized learning at the Regional Lab. The BRL consultants then had to ". . . sell him on the idea of coming, and then get BRL to realize that they really needed him."[8]

New Management

Brian Fitch came to the project in April, 1971, as Don Kendrick's assistant. Kendrick was soon to be transferred to another position within the BRL corporate complex.

In addition to Kendrick's transfer, Clarence Benford transferred to a different elementary school in Gary.

By May, Fitch had "spent seven or eight hours already with the man who will be coming in here as Learning Director."[9] As Fitch put it, ". . . we want to make sure that we're communicating in designing the program, where we are to go and where we are now and what our roles are to be . . . you simply don't make unilateral decisions."[10]

The man Fitch talked about was Sherman Newell, who had been director of the Teacher Corps in Gary.

The styles of Fitch and Newell were more carefully matched for that sensitive dual administrative role than those of Kendrick and Benford had been before them. McAndrew pointed out that ". . . this time around, with Brian and Sherman, we did give a little more thought to the styles and way of operating of these two guys, to make sure we got more of a match."[11]

The match was better, but the jobs of the two men simply were not amenable to description and the first year of the project was not to see a detailed description of the duties and responsibilities of the Center Manager and Learning Director.

BANNEKER

Development *vs.* Demonstration

Under the management of Fitch and Newell, the project made an important accommodation to the pressures on it. The program ceased being touted as a demonstration of a system good enough to guarantee, and began to be talked about, instead, as a joint developmental effort of BRL and School City.

In May, Fitch related:

> Since I've been here in April, I've spent a lot of time getting out to the staff, getting their problem statements, getting their contributions; I'm going to anticipate your question—no independent outfit is simply going to come in and drop a system onto a school. I think that the host school system should realize the staff in the school that is in the performance contract is going to have to work very, very hard in helping to develop that program.[12]

Fitch exhibited the same sort of image to the teachers at Banneker as well. In May, in a covering memorandum for a planning guide for a summer workshop to "consolidate what has been learned during the 1970-1971 school year" was a paragraph that characterized Fitch's approach to change:

> Please feel free to criticize constructively and make suggestions. The attached paper is very general. We will get much more specific in committee meetings as we work together to plan our developmental program. WE ALL NEED TO SHARE OUR IDEAS AND TO WORK TOGETHER! Our goal must be to provide an increasingly better program for each learner and to make it easier for teachers to manage that program.[13]

Several things are important about the image projected by that memorandum in contrast to the management style projected by the previous BRL project director. In addition to "share our ideas" as opposed to "change it like this," it is noteworthy that Fitch's memorandum refers to both the curriculum managers and assistant curriculum managers as teachers as well as managers, though their role is consistently referred to as one of managing.

From December, when Hernandez reported that 11 of the 22 Banneker teachers were probably going to ask for transfer, to May, the situation had changed enough so that no teacher actually asked for a transfer. As one teacher put it:

> Some people have had a rotten year because they didn't like the change. I thought about resigning, but since January, I've changed my mind. . . . I took the transfer thing home and I really thought about it. I had my wife type it out, but since March when they made these changes, I've changed my mind.[14]

In response to the desires of Fitch and McAndrew, and the demands of the "unfavorable situation," BRL sponsored a summer program that employed 18 of the Banneker teachers for the purpose of further developing the individualized system. McAndrew admitted in May that ". . . we didn't really build in enough provision for development input."[15]

The summer development program was in character with what Fitch saw as the roles of the performance contract and the performance contractor:

> The performance contract really provides a basis for negotiations between independent systems developers and school people. What BRL has said is it's responsible, it feels responsible, for the total system development, but it's not just the company materials, it realizes in order to individualize the system, you've got to do more than provide the materials, you've got to provide new cycles and new patterns of movement for children, new scheduling patterns and new staff patterns, and you've got to be able to pull these things together into a cohesive system.[16]

The summer program was intended to help "pull things together into a cohesive system."

BANNEKER

The early, optimistic hopes for the project had been tempered by the first year of operation until at the end of the first school year, Brian Fitch characterized the program this way:

> I think, in the first place, that people who enter this kind of operation have to realize the magnitude of the project they are undertaking, and that you don't merely come in and in a short period of time get things set up. You have several (successive) approximations. I think this year a lot has been accomplished at Banneker. We have a differentiated staffing pattern, we have a nongraded curriculum, and we've got the first approximation of a genuine system of individualized instruction. I think that next year, if all goes according to plan, we will have refined the individualized system even more.[17]

He saw strong value in BRL involvement in the project because in his estimation they had developed an effective reading program and were in the process of developing a math program and ". . . that these systems could be integrated into a total systems approach here, which (gives) BRL a leg up on being able to produce what, in fact, they had promised to produce."[18]

McAndrew said that though Banneker had operated "not without its problems" it looked as if most of the "bugs" were on the way to being solved. He also felt that three years would probably be required before one could tell if performance contracting "in the Banneker pattern" would work.[19]

Ira Judge, a teacher at Banneker, saw the first year, and the prospects for the program, in much the same light. He pointed out in May that:

> McAndrew said in Washington, to some group (the Senate Select Committee on Equal Educational Opportunity) that it's kind of crude and unsophisticated. I think it is. I think next year it is going to be less crude and unsophisticated and the year after that it could be one hell of a program.[20]

The move from emphasizing the demonstration of private

industry's prowess for doing the job, to one of a cooperative developmental project was an accommodation required by both internal and external pressures on the project. In addition, that change seemed to make it much more likely that products and processes useable to other school systems would result from the project.

While by May, 1971, the private postures of the parties involved may have changed considerably from their earlier stances, the public postures of the Union and, for that matter, School City and BRL had not varied greatly.

Even the State Department of Public Instruction (the office changed from OSPI when John Loughlin became Superintendent), while not harrassing the project, were quite cautious about private industry mixing with the public schools.

In July, 1971, in a speech at Indiana University, Loughlin indicated that while "I'm sure there are many fine things that could come out of it," he cautioned about possible "exploitation by private corporations."[21]

Loughlin saw the emphasis on outputs in a favorable light but indicated he would be happier if the projects were developed in the public sector of the economy. He said, "I see no reason why performance contracting projects cannot be developed on this campus, or in the halls of the ISTA (Indiana State Teachers Association), NEA, or AFT."[22]

Evaluation of the First Year

While the payment to BRL was based on norm referenced standardized achievement tests in reading and math, it is beyond the scope of this book to deal with the desirability of using such tests to judge individual gain in achievement. Robert Stake, Henry Dyer, Ralph Tyler, and others, have written much on the subject and generally agree that the norm referenced standardized achievement test is, at best, used inappropriately by performance contractors.

However, there are political reasons for using such tests, even if one were to know that, as Stephen Klein of the Center for the Study of Evaluation at UCLA put it, it is ". . . akin to using the bathroom scales to weigh an air mail letter to find out how much postage is necessary." As Gordon McAndrew put it:

> In fact, for better or worse, or right or wrong, that's the way we do it! We let kids into college based on the SAT, and we let them into graduate school based on the Miller Analogy, and we let them into industry based on all kinds of standardized tests.[23]

While many critics of performance contracting have found the inappropriateness of norm referenced standardized achievement tests to be an attractive weapon to use in attacking various projects, the Gary Teachers' Union argued only about the administration and more particularly the interpretation of the results made by School City.

In a press release dated September 24, 1971, and co-signed by George Stern and Gordon McAndrew, the results of the outside evaluator's (Center for Urban Renewal in Education—CURE) assessment of the first year of the project were made known.

The optimistic interpretation of the results prompted a lengthy analysis by the AFT and GTU that was released on November 5, 1971, as a release with the title *Education vs. Business.*

The School City/BRL release claimed that during the first year "72.5% of the students (546 children in grades 2 through 6) made month for month, or better, gain in reading, mathematics, or both."[24] However, the contract guaranteed month for month gain in *both* reading and mathematics and as the Union analyzed the figures, those students achieving month for month gains in both reading and mathematics represented only 35 percent.[25]

The School City/BRL release also claimed that the "improved performance" was achieved at "no additional cost to the Gary schools."[26] What the release failed to point out was that the savings over the average cost/student in Gary resulted from the penalty paid by BRL for those exiting sixth grade students who had not achieved month for month gains in reading and mathematics.

Differences in interpretation of CURE's results prompted Sandra Irons, the new president of the Gary Teachers' Union, to prepare a press release to parallel the one released by Stern and McAndrew. Both are quoted in full in Panels II and III below:

PANEL II

THE BANNEKER PROGRAM

During the first year of the program at Banneker, 72.5% of the students (546 children in grades two through six) made month for month, or better, gain in reading, mathematics, or both.

The cost/student to the Gary schools was $830. This was almost $100/child less than the $924 spent on each student city-wide.

Prior to the beginning of this new program in September, 1970, Banneker was the next to lowest achieving elementary school in Gary. The average sixth grader was more than a year retarded in reading and mathematics. Seventy five per cent of the school's graduates were below grade level in the fundamental skills. Given the present rate of progress of Banneker students, that statistic will be reversed. Assuming current levels of achievement, we can expect that about 75% of children in the primary grades will graduate from the school performing at or above grade level in reading and/or mathematics. Therefore, while precise statistical treatment of comparative data is not feasible in the first year, there is no doubt that the overall performance of the students has improved. Moreover, this improved performance has been achieved at no additional cost to the Gary schools.

As encouraging as the first year results are, no definitive conclusions can be drawn at this time. Up to now, each effort has gone into organizing this new program and making improvements. The second year at Banneker began this month, and we are optimistic that future results will be even better than those obtained so far. Final evaluation should properly be made at the conclusion of the experiment in 1974.

9/14/71   George McAndrew, Superintendent—Schools
George Stern, President, BRL[27]

PANEL III

THE BANNEKER PROGRAM

During the first year of the program at Banneker, only *35%* of the students (546 children in grades two through six) made month-for-month, or better gains in reading and mathematics.

Prior to the beginning of this new program in September, 1970, Banneker was the third lowest achieving elementary school in Gary and 'seventy-five per cent of the school's graduates were below grade level in the fundamental skills.' The test results from Banneker in September, 1970, indicate that Banneker was 'on the bottom' in reading, and one of two schools 'on the bottom' in mathematics. The mean score for reading was 4.6 and mathematics was 4.7. In June, test results indicate an average five-month gain in reading, and a 1.2 gain in mathematics, and that eighty-one per cent of the school's graduates were below grade level in the fundamental skills.

It is interesting to note that about 60% of the school year was spent on reading and mathematics while other areas were neglected. Yet no appreciable gains were made in reading and mathematics.

While precise statistical treatment of comparative data is not feasible in the first year, there is some doubt that the overall performance of the students has improved. There is further doubt that this lack of improvement has not been an additional cost to the Gary schools.

There are circumstances which lead one to believe that the program was not productive the first year, in that the administrators from last year have been replaced with two new administrators, teachers developed additional materials during the summer, and the enrollment is far below expectancy, despite the intense efforts of the school system to increase the enrollment.

No indication has been given as to the 'money-back guarantee' for the students who were in the program for the one school year (1970-71).

SCI/sad   Sandra C. Irons, President
11/5/71   Gary Teachers' Union, Local No. 4,
       AFT, AFL-CIO[28]

The AFT also released on November 5, 1971, a document with the title *The Banneker Contracted Curriculum Center,* in which they termed the BRL-School City average gain figure of 72.5 percent, a "case of administrative statistic juggling, and a neat public relations job on top of it" and that while striking, the figure was "a calculated deception."[29]

Even after the first year and the internal changes that had occurred in the project, School City and BRL were still claiming that it "costs no more" and the union was still arguing that the project was much more expensive.

While the Union had not been able to scuttle the project, they certainly had not embraced it with open arms. Neither did the State, even with a change of administration, find it desirable to completely accept the performance contract with the outsider.

91

Publicity

Part of the problem of acceptance had to be involved with the national publicity generated by the contract.

"If you do something that does bring an awful lot of attention"—such as the Banneker project—"more attention in terms of publicity than I think is good; it becomes a kind of Roman circus" related McAndrew in May, 1971. "There is a tendency for people to choose up sides, and either to damn it without having seen it, or praising it without having seen it, or really looked at it, and there's a temptation for a board or a superintendent to react, and choose up its own sides. It seems to me it would be very important to try to maintain a sense of balance . . . it is not the answer to man's problems."[30]

McAndrew didn't think it possible to plan for something like the publicity achieved by the Banneker project. In the first place, as he again related in May:

> I don't think I anticipated there would be as much interest in this as there has been; which probably only indicates a kind of desperate seeking for solutions. I think also, it indicates the propensity we have for what may appear to be panaceas. But even with that, and I think we all know that people are looking for some one thing that's going to unlock it. Even knowing that, I have been surprised by the amount of interest expressed, and the amount of reaction pro and con.[31]

Changing the Institution

Even with the detriment of too much publicity, McAndrew saw the outsider as necessary for changing the institution.

> It's a kind of symbolic commitment to be willing to shape up the system, like when you hire a consulting firm to look at your administrative structure, rather than doing it internally. There is some value there—and

some danger—in having an outside guy come in and saying to that guy, look, you're nobody's buddy, you don't owe anybody anything, we're going to pay you so much money, tell us how we ought to organize.[32]

McAndrew saw that as necessary because of the great difficulty he saw in changing institutions. The McAndrew anecdote quoted earlier seems to carry even more importance here:

It's not only the written regulations and the state regulations it's also the institutional inertia; it's not a matter of whether you're forbidden to do something by union agreement, but whether you have the positive thrust to go ahead and do it. I had an experience with one guy who used to work with me who came in here— a very bright guy with all kinds of ideas—and he found himself very frustrated; he'd never worked in a public school bureaucracy. He said, 'it's not that it's forbidden, but when I talk to somebody about doing something different, I'm smothered with kindness, but nothing happens. I can't make the beast move.[33]

McAndrew saw early involvement by all parties as being necessary to the success of any innovative project such as Banneker. He saw the involvement problem as a possible mistake in the Banneker project, but he cautioned ". . . that there is at some point a decision, a management decision, that you have to make—go/no go— because otherwise, . . . there's kind of an institutional reluctance to commit resources in a new direction, and the best way to avoid a decision is to study something."[34] He pointed out that some things have been "under study here" for five years.

The performance contract at Gary died as suddenly and as abruptly as it had been given birth. Though the contract between the School City of Gary and Behavioral Research Laboratories had been signed for a four year period (1970-74), it was only to last for two years, three months, and nine days. Gordon McAndrew announced to the media on December 13, 1972 that the Banneker contract with BRL was to be terminated effective January 1, 1973. In terminating the contract, the school superintendent told

93

reporters, "We've learned what we could from BRL. We'll continue to use many of their procedures. But there is no use having them continue to do what we can now do for ourselves."

With that announcement, the most comprehensive and possibly the most controversial performance contract in the nation was brought to a close.

Gordon McAndrew does not look for more performance contracts in Gary because ". . . as I've said all the way along, if Banneker proves to be viable, we ought to be able to replicate it without the external contractor."[35] That should make both the State and the Union happy.

---

[1] Hernandez, Ernie, "Banneker School a 'Gold Fish Bowl'," *Gary Post-Tribune,* December 20, 1970, p. B-3.

[2] *Ibid.*

[3] Stated by Ira Judge in an interview with the author in May, 1970.

[4] Hall, G. R., and Rapp, M. L., *Case Studies in Educational Performance Contracting,* p. 84.

[5] Judge interview, May, 1970, *op. cit.*

[6] Cray, D. W., "What's Happening in Gary," *School Management,* May, 1971, p. 24.

[7] Stated by Helen Mooney in an interview with the author in May, 1971.

[8] *Ibid.*

[9] Stated by Brian Fitch in an interview with the author in May, 1971.

[10] *Ibid.*

[11] *Ibid.*

[12] Fitch, Brian, Memorandum to Banneker Managers, May 18, 1971.

[13] Judge interview, May, 1970, *op. cit.*

[14] Stated by Gordon McAndrew, Superintendent, School City of Gary, in an interview with the author in May, 1971.

[15] Fitch interview, May, 1971, *op. cit.*

[16] *Ibid.*

[17] *Ibid.*

[18] *Ibid.*

[19] Stated by Gordon McAndrew, Superintendent, School City of Gary, in an interview with the author in March, 1971.

[20] Judge interview, May, 1971, *op. cit.*

[21] Loughlin, J. H., Speech delivered at Indiana University, July 15, 1971.

[22] *Ibid.*

[23] Stated by Gordon McAndrew, Superintendent, School City of Gary, in an interview with the author in January, 1971.

[24] BRL–School City, *The Banneker Program,* Press Release, September 24, 1971.

[25] Gary Teachers' Union, *Education vs. Business,* Press Release, November 5, 1971, p. 3.

[26] *Ibid.*

[27] BRL–School City, *The Banneker Program,* Press Release, September 24, 1971.

[28] Gary Teachers' Union, *Education vs. Business,* Press Release, November 5, 1971, p. 3.

[29] American Federation of Teachers, *The Banneker Contracted Curriculum Center,* November 5, 1971.

[30] McAndrew interview, May, 1971, *op. cit.*

[31] *Ibid.*

[32] *Ibid.*

[33] *Ibid.*

[34] *Ibid.*

[35] *Ibid.*

SIX

CHANGE CAVEATS

Summary

The case materials presented in the first five chapters tell what is basically a simple story. An innovative and ambitious school superintendent got together with an eager young president of an educational technology company and they decided to contract an entire school to that company for four years. The company would guarantee that by the end of the contract each student would be achieving at the national norm or the money spent on his education would be returned, and furthermore, that the contract would be for the same price the school was already spending. This idea, and later its implementation, was enough to engender great hostility on the part of both the local and national teachers' Union and the State Department of Education; the former saw a threat in the changing of teachers' roles (and in the threatened status of teachers) and the latter saw a threat in the forming of new structural relationships which might tend to erode its power. The fierce opposition by the vested interests was not enough to kill the innovation, at least during the first year.

Unfortunately, the superintendent and the company president were dealing with an innovation that wasn't quite ready to go. This fact, and the pressure of the opposition, caused accommodations in the innovation that had the effect of bringing it back toward the status quo. Nevertheless, even though the school, after the first year, wasn't quite as different as had been predicted, no one could deny the superintendent his victory over the opposition, and the innovation was to receive its chance to prove its effectiveness.

BANNEKER

Questions raised by the case. Many questions come easily to
mind when one considers this case. Is it likely to be repeated?
Must the Union always find itself in opposition to any innovation
that concerns the organizational structures of an entire school?
Must the Union always lose in its opposition to innovations that
prescribe new roles for professional teachers, paraprofessionals,
students, and materials in the management of educational enter-
prises? Must the State always find itself in opposition to innovations that prescribe new organizational structures and use methods
and materials not prescribed by State regulation? Must the State
always lose in any attempt to maintain the status quo through
enforcement of its rules and regulations? Must innovations always
make accommodations so that the innovation is more like the
status quo, in order to defend itself against its opposition? Must
private industry always guarantee innovations and price them so
that they cost no more than standard practice in order to overcome the opposition generated by tampering with existing organizational patterns and structures? It would be simple-minded and
completely misleading if one were to try to provide answers to
these questions through the analysis of a single case.

It might be possible to predict the fate of future attempts to
diffuse the same type of innovation from the Gary story, but only
if all the conditions were to be the same. The State Superintendent
of Public Instruction would have to be a lame duck and at odds
politically with even those in his own party; the Governor would
have to be on the side of the innovation and against those who
would stop it; the question of race would have to be a part of the
innovation; the school superintendent would have to have his
board solidly on his side in the controversy, and be bright, tough,
and determined in the bargain; the Union would have to have been
somewhat emaciated by a strike during the previous year and have
the reputation of being white dominated in an increasingly black
dominated community; the national press would have to be not
only in attendance during the early stages of the innovation but
positively impressed by it as well; a company would have to be in
a position to invest resources far beyond what they could hope to
recoup on site; and society would have to be supportive of almost
any innovation purporting to help black kids learn better. This
isn't to say that all these conditions must be met for a similar

innovation to succeed, it is only to say that to be able to predict the success of future attempts to diffuse similar innovations from this single case would require that all these conditions, and more, be met.

While the results of the first year of the performance contract in Gary, when stripped to the basics, make a relatively simple story, when one attends to the power relationships, the configurations of the various groups involved, the linkages between and among those groups, and the resources available for the innovation and for those that were in the position of defending the status quo, one finds that the story rapidly becomes much more complex than the simplified results would indicate. The best that can be hoped for from the analysis of this case is to tentatively explain why what happened happened. With the complexity of the story and the size of the stage on which it played, any theory used to provide structure for analysis must be broad enough to provide structure for analyzing not only what happened in a single school, but must be capable of including analysis of a total school system, the effects of a state department of public instruction, the effects of a national and local union, and even any effect of the national press.

Accurate prediction of future events might well be the acid test of any theory within a well developed "hard" science. But it certainly is too much to expect of a "science" as young as that concerned with organizational aspects affecting educational change. Perhaps analysis can help direct the focus of those interested in change on those elements in the system that are most conducive to changing an organization.

This alone would provide a great advance over the standard way of thinking about innovation in education, that is, if you build a better mousetrap the world will beat a path to your door. Of course, the efficacy of any proposed innovation is to be taken into account, but it would be naive to believe that a "good" innovation is enough, or even the most important element in the equation of change.

In order for this case to be more than a description of an isolated change event, it might be desirable to use a theoretical structure in an attempt to analyze the interactions between the units in the suprasystem made up by the organizations in question.

99

BANNEKER

A structure for analysis. There are many different models and theories of educational change available in the literature. The theory that seemed to offer the most promise in analyzing this case is the *Configurational Theory of Innovation Diffusion* developed by Bhola.[1] This theory deals with planned change and is broad enough to be able to encompass the setting of the performance contract in Gary. As Bhola says about his theory:

> The crux of this theory is a classification for configurations of change in terms of the social units involved as innovators and adopters; thus enabling change agents to choose a relative perspective with regard to a particular change situation and to bring forth a specific level of response if change intervention is to be made.

> A second important idea proposed in the theory is that the occurrence or the nonoccurrence of a change event would depend upon four things; (1) the type and quality of the relationship between the change makers and the target of change; (2) the linkages within and between these two parties; (3) the social environment around them; and (4) the resources available to the change makers for making the change and to the adopters for adopting the changes being offered to them. To increase the probability of a change event to occur a change agent must optimize these four factors.[2]

The statements above related to innovators-adopters can be expanded to include resistors or competing innovator groups. This expansion allows the theory to serve the analysis of the Banneker story usefully, as the working equation in this case is more nearly initiator-resistor than initiator-adopter.

It deserves to be pointed out here that a knowledge of the most important elements to be attended to during any attempt to change an organization could serve those who would defend the status quo just as well as it could serve those who would change the organization. Change theories should not be thought of as the private property of those who would change educational organizations, as they could be useful to anyone having the responsibility for leading an educational organization or providing leadership for educational organizations from any capacity.

Bhola's equation to be used in attempting to explain the Banneker case is $D = f(C,L,E,R)$; where D is the probability of the diffusion of an innovation; C is the configurational relationship between the initiator and the target of an innovation; L is the type and extent of the linkage between and within configurations; E is the environment in which the configurations are located; and R indicates the resources available to the configurations for enhancing or diminishing the probability of the innovation being integrated into the target system. In simple terms, when C,L,E, and R are optimized, the probability of the innovation being integrated into the target system is maximized.

Theoretical explanation. In attempting to analyze the first year of the Banneker performance contract, the first item on the agenda is the make-up of the innovation. Just as the situation of the performance contract is complex, the innovation is complex. It would be much simpler to deal with a single tool or technique as the innovation rather than, as is the case here, a whole new set of tools and techniques as well as new decision making structures and new roles for both teachers and students. The innovation in this case is part programmed instruction, part differentiated staffing, part nongraded curriculum, part emphasis on the three R's and part a systems approach to school. In order to be able to attempt to integrate the changes listed above, BRL found it necessary to provide for many other changes as well, changes like providing new cycles and patterns of movement for the students and new managerial patterns. But the basic thrust of this innovation turns out to be *structural* and implies the making up of a whole new set of roles and the rules for relating those roles.

The original proposal called for almost complete delegation of authority from the Board to BRL. Formal accommodation was made early on this point; however, the Center Manager provided by the company maintained much control for the company because he had a great deal of clout in determining the day-to-day activities at Banneker. Although School City provided a Learning Director, the company kept the lion's share of the control in the beginning. The Learning Director's role was clearly subservient to that of the Center Manager and, in fact, the learning directors' role more nearly approximated that of an assistant Principal than that of a Principal.

The performance contract provided for considerable change in role for the teachers. The management aspect of teaching was greatly emphasized as were the materials. The teacher no longer decided when, where, and how to use materials, rather it was the materials, tests, and students that almost decided when, where, and how to use the teachers. Rather than being teaching aides, the materials became so important that one member of the School City central staff was able to say about the teachers that ". . . they more or less monitor learning, rather than involve themselves deeply in it, you see, just because you are working with, for the most part, programmed materials."[3] When one considers the role change for the teachers; the imposition of the new role of the paraprofessional; and the new emphasis on student success that blames the system (including the teacher) if the student fails to achieve up to expectations, it becomes quite obvious why the Union felt constrained to attempt to block this innovation. The fact that the company strongly implied that they would be able to do a better job, at a cheaper price, using a much lower proportion of professional teachers made the threat from the performance contract even stronger.

If we have some idea what the innovation was, we still need to make some determination of the constitution of the innovator, adopter, and resistors. The innovator is most easily described. The initiator system is made up of the company (BRL), the sponsor, McAndrew, and the financers, School Board. There are other individuals involved in this function, but the major actors are those described.

The adopter system could be seen to consist of students, parents, and teachers. The adopter system was passive and did not figure much in this change event. The students are acted upon by the innovation, but they have no real power to affect the system, so are easily overlooked when decisions are made. The parents of the students have more power, though it is usually dormant. The innovator was careful to sell the community before the innovation even appeared on the scene. The publicity that the company had ways to help black kids learn better and that they were so proud of these ways that they were willing to give a money-back guarantee, made the innovation very attractive to the community. The fact that they were hiring parents to be paraprofessionals and taking only those from the immediate community for that job seemed to be enough to complete the elimination of the immediate community as a major source of concern.

One could consider the teachers also to be a part of the adopter system, but several factors militated against thinking that the teachers have much real say in determining whether this innovation was to be integrated into the system or thrown off by the system. One important factor was that the teachers were interviewed before the contract began for the purpose of determining who would stay at Banneker and who would be declared "surplus" and transferred to other schools. In order to be able to stay at Banneker, the teachers had already given at least tacit approval to the project. In any case, the teachers, working for the Board, were at least formally constrained to accept the project and work for its success.

However, in this case study, one can describe much more clearly the configurations capable of being resistors. Though individual teachers might have found themselves incapable of mounting any serious resistance to the innovation due to the factors described above and the additional factor of the scarcity of teaching positions during the time of the project, they could mount some collective resistance to the proposed structural and role changes through their Union. The Union was not in the position of adopting or failing to adopt the innovation, but it was in a powerful enough position that it could provide effective resistance against the adoption of the innovation.

The major ally of the Union in its resistance against the adoption of the innovation was the State Department of Public Instruction. The State saw immediately that the proposed delegation of authority to a private company could dilute the State's power and control over the education of the Banneker students. Though one elementary school of more than 2,000 schools would hardly be worth the level of resistance provided by the State, the fact that structural changes were involved that could provide precedent was enough to generate a high level of resistance to this particular innovation. The State could see that though it might

103

retain all its legal power, it would not have any effective linkage between it and the company through which to exercise this legal power. The developed linkages were between the State and the local school administration, and if the company were to be in control of Banneker, the State would have to develop new structures and new relationships in order to be able to discharge its constitutional responsibility.

The adopter system then, if one considers the teachers, the parents, and the students at Banneker to make up the adopter system, does not figure significantly in the equation. Essentially, the innovator configuration was composed of the company, the School City central administration, and the Gary School Board. The resistor configurations were the State and the Union, sometimes working separately and sometimes together, but constantly working to prevent any rules from being changed. It is interesting enough to note here that the disturbance of the status quo was not provided through the provision of new or unusual goals; on the contrary, the goals embraced by the performance contract were quite conventional, even conservative goals. The emphasis was on achievement rather than self-understanding, the three R's rather than fine arts or liberal education, and on discipline rather than self-expression. The goals certainly were not unusual enough to cause all the ruckus that ensued, but the changes foreseen in the various organizational structures clearly were.

Power relationships between configurations. Where decisions are to be contested, power is the implicit variable. When innovations in education are considered, the decision to accept or reject an innovation is, in many cases, made, not on the basis of benefit to the student or efficient use of the taxpayer's money, but rather on the basis of which of the vested interests can muster the most useable power. Any description of the configurations involved in this event would be incomplete without some indication not only of the legal power to act, but of the informal political power available to the configurations as well.

Those groups making up the innovator configuration, the board, the company, and the local administration, held legal power over the budget. In addition they had the acceptance of the local community of the innovation, the power of the mayor (who appoints the Board), and encouragement from the national press in their favor.

The power of the innovator configuration was certainly not total, as the innovation in question was not fully developed, and found itself open to criticism by those in opposition to it. The rather simplistic goals and the undeveloped methods of testing for the achievement of those goals both were somewhat vulnerable. The company's first manager of the center exhibited a serious lack of understanding of the culture of the school and of the role expectations of the teachers. He appeared to be uncomfortably authoritarian in his dealings with both teachers and paraprofessionals. This resulted in charges of dictatorship which tended to erode some of the press and community support enjoyed by the innovation. The company and the central administration of the school were able to make accommodations in the innovation to overcome many of the negative effects mentioned, but it must be pointed out that they had no real choice but to make significant accommodations in order for the innovation to continue. The prime example of this fact was the shift in public statements from the earlier implication that this was a demonstration that a private company could perform schooling better and at no extra cost, to later statements which asserted that the company and School City were involved in a joint developmental effort that could ultimately improve schools.

While the power available to the initiator configuration was not total, that configuration did make excellent use of the formal and informal power available to it.

The State has legal final authority over any action involving violation of State rule or regulation. The violation of State rules and regulations is important to consider because, since structural relationships in education are defined, in most cases, by State rules and regulations, any innovation that significantly changes structural relationship, is automatically in violation.

Though the State held the legal authority, it found the use of this power to be blunted somewhat by political considerations. The State Superintendent, during the final conflicts over the project, was a lame duck. The incoming administration was thought to favor the innovation and even though the Governor was of the same political party as the Superintendent, he had indicated, in the press, acceptance of the innovation and had implied the threat to overturn any negative action by the Superintendent regarding the innovation. The State Superintendent also found it uncomfortable to be cast as being opposed to progress, and even more uncomfortable to be against an innovation that was purported to help give black kids a better chance to learn. One indication of the position the State Superintendent found himself in was his attempt to buy the innovation off by offering $20,000 from his contingency fund to Gary for the purpose of hiring a BRL consultant without the performance contract and its attendant changing of the structural relationships between the State and local school governments. Gary was able to refuse this offer because of the power they held.

The Union held the power of almost total membership of the local teachers (about 98 percent) but they found their power to be completely blunted by other considerations. The Union had struck during the year previous to the inauguration of the performance contract. The strike had left their community support in question as well as having their membership reluctant to strike again so soon over something that was not perceived as a direct and immediate threat to employment. The fact that the contract was in effect at only one of the many elementary schools and was touted by the administration as an experimental effort only, was also a disadvantage in encouraging action as serious as another strike among the Union membership. The fact that Indiana did not have a collective bargaining act that would allow the Union to sue for breach of contract limited the Union's power to the threat of strike and to the gathering of local and press support to shame the administration into honoring what was only an agreement rather than a contract between the Union and the Board. The fact that all the Banneker students and almost all the Banneker teachers were black also figured in the Union's consideration of actions, as the Union had the reputation in the community of being a white dominated organization. This made it doubly difficult to be in opposition to an innovation publicized as helping black children to learn better. The Gary Teachers' Union did have the moral support at the national AFT, but that support was limited to attempting to sway the national press from their encouragement of the idea of performance contracting.

Linkages. In commenting about the linkages important to this innovation, 10 linkages are listed and each very briefly discussed as to how they were effectively manipulated by the initiator configuration. There obviously were more possible permutations than 10, but these were perceived by the author as being the most important to this case. The order is not meant to imply any ranking, either in importance or complexity. The initiator configuration found its major spokesman and prime contact with other configurations in the person of Gordon McAndrew. It should be remembered that when the initiator configuration was mentioned that Gordon McAndrew was not only the chief executive officer of the Board, but that he had major control over the interactions of that entire configuration.

1. *State-Initiator.* It was to the initiator's advantage to keep this linkage as ineffective as possible since the State held all the legal power. McAndrew was able to do this by avoiding meetings called by Superintendent Wells, much to Wells' consternation, and by avoiding even the answering of his telephone when the occasion demanded. The need to keep this particular linkage in disarray might be the reason that the Initiator failed to ask the State for even those waivers of rules that were usually granted on request (i.e., textbook waivers for experimental materials). The State, on the other hand, made attempts to articulate this linkage, publicly complaining that McAndrew hadn't shown up at the General Commission meetings that dealt with the Banneker question. In order to keep this linkage in disorder, McAndrew seemed to keep shifting the responsibility around among his staff so that the State had to deal with new people as often as possible. These new people could claim lack of understanding of the State's directions thereby gaining time for the innovation to continue. When the communications became critical to the project from the initiator's point of view, during the hearing to recommission the school, McAndrew did show up at the State Board meeting, but his appearance was the exception rather than the rule.

2. *Initiator-Banneker.* One could have as many linkages to Banneker as there were people at Banneker, but for the purpose

of this discussion, we considered the more abstract configuration as the agent in communication. During the early stages of the project, it was mediated by the company as most of the communicating was done through BRL's man. During the month of December, Gordon McAndrew began to get information that all was not well at Banneker and he made a day's tour talking directly with teachers and students. The information gained on this momentary improvement of the quality of this linkage was to serve as the basis for talks, discussions, and decisions during the Christmas break. McAndrew was to look back on the Christmas discussions as having been critical to the continuance of the project. During the later stages of the first year the central administration began to communicate more with their own man at Banneker and this linkage improved.

3. *State–Banneker.* It was to the initiator's advantage to keep this linkage from being formed too well early in the project. The investigators from the State complained of being "shepherded" through Banneker. During the later stages of the project when accommodations had been made in the project, this linkage lost importance. When Banneker began to welcome investigators from the State they lost interest in going there.

4. *Initiator–Union.* The formality required in this linkage was an important factor. The Union president spoke of his desire to have other people in attendance when he talked with Superintendent McAndrew. Moreover, most communication was through rather formal and legalistic letters and memoranda. Since the Union had little direct power over the Initiator, this linkage was not particularly important either to McAndrew or the Union. The linkage between the press and the Union was of much more importance to the Union as they seemed to see that linkage as their link with the community.

5. *Union–Banneker.* In the early stages of the project, it was to the Initiator's advantage to keep this linkage from being of high quality, but the risk involved in attempting to keep the Union out of any single school was simply too great. Thus, the Union was allowed free access to the project at all times. During the early stages of this investigation, the Union president offered the author access to Banneker through the Union, should he have difficulty gaining entrance. The Union president was a good source of

information about Banneker during the early stages of the project, but during the latter part of the first year the Union had apparently lost interest in the project as accommodations were achieved. During one of the author's trips to Gary, the Union president offered to buy lunch if he were told what was going on at Banneker since he said he had not had the time lately to follow it very closely. Banneker had clearly fallen to a low level on his priority list.

6. *Union–Press.* This linkage was important to the Union and every attempt was made to cooperate with the press. The national Union helped do research for the preparation of press releases and in fact formed a strong link with the national press for the purpose of disseminating information about performance contracting, including the Banneker contract. Of course, what was "information" to the Union was propaganda from the Initiator's point of view.

7. *Press–Banneker.* The attempt was strongly made to keep this linkage very carefully controlled, particularly during the early stages of the project. As accommodations were made in the project the control was relaxed, until before the end of the first year of the project the national press, at least, was welcomed openly and allowed to roam the project at will.

8. *Press–Initiator.* While the Initiator group used the press to disseminate information favorable to the project, they also felt the need to keep this linkage providing accurate information during the troubled stages of the project. Examples of carefully engineered press releases that did more to confuse than to clarify are evidenced in the case materials.

9. *Press–State.* This linkage was not at all well developed. The State knew what the press was reporting, but the press apparently had little interest in what the State had to say on the subject and the State made little attempt to improve this linkage.

10. *Banneker–Other Gary Elementary Schools.* Though the proposal provided for various techniques of involving other Gary schools in the Banneker project so that they may come to understand the techniques and methods used in this project, this linkage was interesting because of its almost complete absence. The case was made by the Initiator configuration that the project was experimental and any decision to diffuse any methods or techniques among the other Gary schools must wait for an assessment

of the success of the performance contract at Banneker. While this may well be the case, the Initiator must have also realized that the less well developed this linkage was, the less threatening this change would be viewed by the other elementary school teachers in Gary.

It must be obvious by now that the optimization of linkages from the Initiator's point of view was not always the same as maximizing the quality of the linkage. In order to increase the probability of getting the innovation integrated into the system, some linkages needed to be of the highest quality possible, while others must be disrupted in order to be favorable to the innovation.

Environment. While the environment of this particular innovation was undoubtedly important to its success, the environment is relatively simple to explain. During the first year of this project, civil rights for blacks was a major national issue. Moreover, equal opportunity for an education was a national issue as well, providing a favorable environment for any innovation claiming to help black children better learn. Couple that issue with the talk by the national administration about "accountability" in education, and its high regard for the business ethic, one finds that a favorable national environment for the performance contracting notion is established.

The fact that Gary was experiencing serious budget problems, was becoming increasingly black dominated, and had an innovative school administration facing problems of underachievement on standardized tests by its black student population was enough to suggest that an innovation offering to increase standardized test scores at no extra cost and with a guarantee, had to find a favorable local acceptance.

Resources. The power resources of the various configurations have been delineated in describing those configurations, but there were other resources to be reckoned with. The lack of financial resources of the Gary school system was important in their decision to accept an innovation that offered to do a better job at no increased cost, because no matter how good the innovation, if it had cost more, the school system would simply have had to turn it down because of their serious financial problems. The guarantee offered by the company minimized the political risk involved in innovation. If it failed, it was the fault of the company, not the local administration. Moreover, the company would have to give back the money spent on the innovation.

The company could afford to provide resources beyond any possible return on site because they were in the process of "buying in" to a new market for their products and expertise. They could also write off the additional resources required as developmental costs for new products, as well as exposure and publicity costs. The company could afford to assume the risk in order to advertise the faith they had in the effectiveness of their materials.

While both the State and the Union were somewhat low in political resources, they did have enough influence resources to force some accommodation by the school district and the company.

The resource part of the equation of change was strongly in favor of the project.

The project began with real structural changes; teachers found themselves in a different role in relation to students, materials, paraprofessionals, and their supervisors. They found that they had little to say in decisions about process until toward the end of the first year. Accommodations made by the project moved the structures back so that they were more nearly normal. The principal was able to retrieve some control, and the teachers were able to increase their control through their curriculum managers. The company took a less dominant role by, in part, the hiring of a Center Manager that maintained a much lower profile. The traditional structure was reasserted itself, but changes remained. Attitudes about the purpose of schools, the role of school administration, the role of teachers, the role of students, and the role of materials were some of the changes remaining at the end of the first year.

The battle over Banneker was fought on legalistic and structural grounds. The project threatened to change the structures and since the structures are defined, in large part, by rules and regulations, the battle was over rules and regulations. It deserves to be reiterated that in order to significantly change the various structures in a school organization, the rules and regulations must be changed, waived, or violated.

Conclusions

It must be remembered that any conclusions drawn from this single case and its analysis about possible diffusion of performance contracting, or the more general question of change within the educational system can, at the very best, be only tentative. Though, recognizing that the exercise is speculative, it still can be worthwhile to attempt to draw conclusions relating directly to the structural aspects of performance contracting and schools from this in-depth investigative experience with one such subject. One further caution is that we are unlikely to ever find, to use Bhola's Configurational Theory, C,L,E, and R, arrayed exactly as they have been in this case.

First, speculations about the future of performance contracting as exhibited at Banneker:

1. Performance contracting can only become widespread if a State permits it. Any State Department is likely to be reluctant to allow the linkages between the State Department and the local schools to be confused by the intrusion of a third party into that structure.

2. The State will almost always have legal authority on its side in any controversy involving performance contracting, at least as performance contracting was exhibited at Banneker, because part of the innovation is the changing of some of the organizational structures that are defined by State rules and regulations.

3. In order to be attractive on a large scale to profit-making companies, performance contracting must save money on salaries to be able to emphasize the role of materials in the education process. The initiator, therefore, must find any collective organization of teachers less than enthusiastic about the prospects of the outsider coming in and violating not only the role expectations of its membership, but the employment of its membership as well.

4. The educational goals of performance contracted projects are likely to be limited to rather conservative, basic education goals due to the present limitations of the kind of achievement tests readily accepted by the public.

5. Performance contracting in the Banneker mold seems to

require that the outsider invest more resources than he can reasonably hope to gain from the site of the contract.

6. In order to be attractive to school systems from a resource point of view, it seems that performance contractors must either invest some of their own resources or violate the organizational structures of schools to an extent likely to engender strong resistance from the educational community. If performance contracting with a party outside the traditional school structure is to continue, it likely will be only on a pilot, demonstration, or developmental basis, rather than becoming integrated into American public education on any large scale.

Recognizing that generalizing about change in education from the experience of a single case is, at best, questionable, there are, nevertheless, some very tentative conclusions which can be drawn from the Gary experience. If the preceding and following tentative conclusions do no more than direct attention to problems inherent in innovation diffusion which, heretofore, have received insufficient attention, they will have well served their purpose.

A few tentative conclusions about change in education from the Banneker experience follow:

1. Role expectations were strong, and any innovation in this area can expect to meet strong resistance unless it has a well developed new reward system to make it attractive to the population affected by the changes.

2. Innovations that tamper with the organizational structures of schools should expect to see their innovations make the kind of accommodations that will tend to return them to the status quo. The accommodations will likely come either from the Initiator in response to vested interest pressure, or, informally, from the staff as they massage their role in order that it more nearly meets their expectations of it.

3. Until the method of financing public education is changed, innovators must offer resource advantages to schools in order for their innovation to be attractive enough to be adopted on any large scale. To be better is not enough; it must also be cheaper.

4. Since the major portion of resources available for public education goes to salaries, any large scale innovation that meets the criterion of resource advantage for the schools

can expect to find strong resistance from teacher organizations.

5. Innovators that plan changes that directly or indirectly cause changes in the organizational structures within schools should plan tactics for dealing with State Departments of Education. If the innovation causes significant changes in organizational structures or the linkages between schools and State departments, it will, in all likelihood, be illegal. State Department of Education rules and regulations, in this case, must then be changed, waived, or violated.

Recommendations

The author agrees with Sarason that:

> The knowledgeable reader will know that important aspects of the school can only be comprehended by examining the formal and informal relationships between a school system and the state department of education, a set of relationships that leads one into the legislative process and, of course, politics in the narrow sense.[4]

The State Department of Education is important, usually in the negative sense, to any experimental project that tampers with the school organization. But it is absolutely critical, again usually in the negative sense, to the spread of any innovative project having to do with the school organization. The blocking of an innovation, of course, can be good, bad, or indifferent, depending on the innovation in question, but those with an interest in any innovation of the type mentioned should know the usual effect of State Departments of Education.

While more case studies of the actual functioning of schools are needed, it seems equally important that broad theories of educational change, such as the Configurational Theory, need to be applied to sets of case materials in order to discover any regularities existing in changing educational organizations. The conceptual theories applied for this purpose must be broad enough to encompass the large stage—not only of an entire school, but the total school system, and even the state department of education.

In addition to the two basic areas mentioned above, several other likely areas for further research can be mentioned:

1. The effectiveness of internal versus external change agents seems to offer an area for further investigation. Can the beast be made to move best from the inside or from the outside?

2. Does an innovation always require a "sponsor" to become integrated into the system? Must that sponsor always be the superintendent?

3. The problems caused by the early euphoria of innovation need to be studied. Are there ways to hold early expectations of effectiveness and early expectations of the time required to "shake down" an innovation to reasonable levels and still generate the positive thrust necessary to change the organization?

4. The difference between planning for the diffusion of innovative devices (e.g., computers, teaching machines, etc.) and new ways of organizing schools (e.g., building autonomy, performance contracting, etc.) seems to need careful study.

5. The development of new reward systems that encourage change and experimentation in the organizational structures that make up schools needs thought and study.

Many researchers are devoting much effort to developing new devices, methods, and techniques for making education more effective, more enjoyable, more relevant to the needs of the students, and less expensive. This most important task, however, can result in little of value unless these devices, ideas, and techniques are integrated into education, and, as the Banneker story indicates, this is no easy task. We know only a little about how to attempt it. We need to know more.

---

[1] Bhola, H. S., "The Configurational Theory of Innovation Diffusion," *Indian Educational Review* 2(1)42-72, 1967.

[2] Bhola, H. S., "Configurations of Change," 1972, pp. 1-2.

[3] Moscove, Francine, "The Experiment at Banneker School," *Writer's Workshop Pamphlet No. 3,* May, 1971, p. 6.

[4] Sarason, S. B., *The Culture of the School and the Problem of Change,* p. 234.

BIBLIOGRAPHY

American Federation of Teachers, *The Banneker Contracted Curriculum Center,* November 5, 1971, 9 pp.

Anderson, Monroe, "Private Company Runs a Public School to Boost Kids Learning," *The National Observer,* October 26, 1970, p. 6.

"Banneker at Bay," *Newsweek,* March 15, 1971, p. 95.

"Banneker Cut-off Effects 'Nothing'—McAndrew," *Gary Post-Tribune,* February 19, 1971, p. B-1.

Berson, Minnie P., "Interview with Donald Kendrick," in *Journal of the Association of Childhood Education,* March, 1971.

Bhola, H. S., "The Configurational Theory of Innovation Diffusion," *Indian Educational Review* 2(1):42-72, 1967.

Bidwell, Charles E., "The School as a Formal Organization," *Handbook of Organizations,* Rand McNally, 1965, 1,247 pp.

Cray, Douglas, "What's Happening in Gary?" *School Management,* May, 1971, p. 24.

Hall, G. R., and Rapp, M. L., *Case Studies in Educational Performance Contracting,* The Rand Corporation, Santa Monica, California, December, 1971, 110 pp.

Hall, George R., and Stucker, James P., "The Rand/HEW Study of Performance Contracting in Education," Education Commission of the States, January, 1971, 11 pp.

116

Havelock, Ronald G., *et al.*, *Planning for Innovation Through Dissemination and Utilization of Knowledge,* University of Michigan Press, Ann Arbor, 1971, 526 pp.

Hernandez, Ernie, "McAndrew, Union Meet on Grievance," *Gary Post-Tribune,* October 29, 1970, p. A-8.

"Banneker School a 'Gold Fish Bowl,' " *Gary Post-Tribune,* December 10, 1970, p. B-3.

"Arbitration on Banneker is Continued," *Gary Post-Tribune,* January 21, 1971, p. B-2.

McAndrew, Gordon, "Can Institutions Change?" *Educational Leadership,* January, 1970, pp. 354-358.

McCarty, Donald J., and Ramsey, Charles E., *The School Managers, Power and Conflict in American Education,* Greenwood Publishers, Westport, Connecticut, 1971, 281 pp.

Maslow, A. H., "Observing and Reporting Educational Experiments," *Humanist,* January-February, 1965, p. 13.

Mecklenburger, James A., and Wilson, John A., "The Performance Contract in Gary," *Phi Delta Kappan* LII:406-410, March, 1971.

"The Performance Contracts in Grand Rapids," *Phi Delta Kappan* LII:590-594, June, 1971.

"Learning C.O.D.: Can the Schools Buy Success?" *Saturday Review,* September 18, 1971, pp. 62-65, 76-79.

"Performance Contracting in Cherry Creek?" *Phi Delta Kappan,* September, 1971, pp. 51-54.

"Behind the Scores at Gary," *Nation's Schools* 88:28-29, December, 1971.

BIBLIOGRAPHY

Moscove, Francine, "The Experiment at Banneker School," *Writer's Workshop Pamphlet No. 3,* May, 1971, 20 pp.

"Performance Contracting: Why the Gary School Board Bought It. And How," *American School Board Journal,* January, 1971, p. 21.

Sarason, Seymour B., *The Culture of the School and the Problem of Change,* Boston, Allyn and Bacon, 1971, 246 pp.

Scott, Richard W., "Field Methods in the Study of Organizations," *Handbook of Organizations,* Rand McNally, 1965, 1,247 pp.

Sigel, Efrem, and Sobel, Myra, *Accountability and the Controversial Role of the Performance Contractors,* Knowledge Industry Publications, White Plains, New York, February, 1971, 93 pp.

Smith, Vernon H., "Alternative Schools: A Rationale for Action," *Changing Schools,* No. 002, 1972, 21 pp.

"Stockton and Gary Portray Two Views on Contracting," *Education Daily,* April 1, 1971.

"Whitcomb Asks Study of School Ban," *The Indianapolis Star,* February 20, 1971, p. A-4.

"Teaching for Profit," *Newsweek,* August 17, 1970, p. 58.

Zuckerman, Ed, "Banneker 'Report Card' in Works," *Gary Post-Tribune,* September 15, 1971, p. B-1.

INDEX

INDEX